india
style

Monisha Bharadwaj

with photography by Bharath Ramamrutham

SOMA

This book is for Nitish, Arrush, and Saayli—with all my love and thanks for your support, patience, and generosity.

Text © 1998 Monisha Bharadwaj
Photography © 1998 Bharath Ramamrutham

First published 1998 by Kyle Cathie Limited. North American edition published 1999 by SOMA Books, by arrangement with Kyle Cathie.

SOMA Books is an imprint of Bay Books & Tapes,
555 De Haro St., No. 220, San Francisco, CA 94107.

For the Kyle Cathie edition:
Editor: Kate Oldfield
Designer: Paul Welti
Production: Lorraine Baird

For the SOMA edition:
Publisher: James Connolly
Production: Jeff Brandenburg
North American Editor: Heather Garnos

Library of Congress Cataloging-in-Publication Data

Bharadwaj, Monisha.
     India Style / Monisha Bharadwaj ;
  with photography by Bharath Ramamrutham
         p.   cm.
     Previously published: London: Kyle Cathie, Ltd., 1998.
     Includes bibliographical references and index.
     ISBN 1-57959-052-7
     1. Interior decoration--India. I. Ramamrutham, Bharath.
  II. Title
  NK2076.A1B53   1999
  747.2954--dc21   99–14617
                                              CIP

ISBN 1-57959-052-7
Printed in Singapore
10 9 8 7 6 5 4 3 2 1

Distributed by Publishers Group West

contents

introduction

what is indian style?

India is a land of glorious flamboyance and excess. Step into this vast subcontinent and the senses are suffused with a riot of vibrant colors, earth-rich smells, tingling tastes, and a tapestry of textures and sounds.

Celebrations of festivals, wedding processions, and election campaigns are all larger-than-life events that call for public participation and collective self-expression. It is this common spirit of India that unites the whole nation, bridges linguistic and cultural divides and geographical boundaries, and lends a unique identity to the very heart and soul of the country.

There is a tremendous diversity among the people of India, as there is bound to be in a nation of some 900 million. The majority, around 85 percent, are Hindu, while the 76 million Muslims, concentrated in the north, constitute the third largest Muslim population in the world. Christianity and Judaism came to India centuries ago, and while Judaism is in terminal decline, Christianity took hold, especially in the south, where it remains strong. The Parsees traveled from Persia to India around 1,200 years ago. The influence of this prosperous but shrinking religion can be seen everywhere, since this philanthropic community used much of the money it made in business and trade to build hospitals and colleges and to patronize the arts. And last but certainly not least are the Sikhs, the highly religious Jains, and the Buddhists.

a diverse nation

With twenty-five states, fourteen official languages, hundreds of dialects, and more than thirty recognized political parties, India is an enormous melting pot of lifestyles and customs. It is impossible to generalize about such a vast country, where many of the states are larger than most European nations.

ornamentation

There are, though, a few characteristics that bind the whole nation together. One that immediately springs to mind is the people's love of ornamentation. Every village, town, and city has superlative examples of artistry and craftsmanship, and it isn't just homes, clothes, and public spaces that offer themselves up for embellishment: every surface is a candidate for decoration. Even Indian lorries are gaudily painted, sporting vibrant blue peacocks and shocking pink lotuses and the delightfully polite phrase, "Horn please, OK?" And decoration extends beyond the visual: taxis, vans, and trucks play electronic versions of *Für Elise* or *Jingle Bells* when backing up to warn pedestrians of their approach.

At every turn the senses are suffused with a profusion of sights, sounds, smells, and textures.

Color adds sparkle to everyday life. A painted ceiling in Kutch (above) is a good example. A galaxy of Diwali lanterns herald India's grandest Hindu celebration of light (right).

Yet despite the vast range of form and influence, in every design—be it in a public building in Calcutta, a simple bed cover in a Gujarati mud hut, or just the way a young girl dresses in Mahabalipuram—there will always be a distinctive motif, a particular flourish, or a telling use of color that marks the style firmly as Indian.

eclectic assimilation

India is a country blessed by benevolent gods. However, the tranquil and at times awe-inspiring scenery belies the bloody history of the sub-continent, constantly ravaged by marauding foreign powers and divided by internal factions. After each battle for independence from foreign rule, India has survived and assimilated some of the culture that was introduced with external conquest. Islamic, Portuguese, British, and other conquerors left nuances of their language, way of life, cuisine, and architecture, which took root and flowered along with the indigenous style, giving rise to a strange but beautiful hybrid form—a form that is now so comfortably settled in India that the original influences are no longer easily discernible.

the home as a temple

All Indians are innately proud of their homes, and most consider them temples for the mind and body—places where physical and spiritual cleansing and nourishment can occur. Most aspects of life, including the construction and decoration of homes, are governed by traditional customs, practices, and rituals. Anyone who walks into a Hindu home on a special occasion will in all likelihood be treated to a welcome fit for royalty. The housewife will

festoon the main entrance with garlands of flowers and mango leaves, draw elaborate patterns on the floor, and light an oil lamp of welcome. As her guests stand at the threshold, she will apply the *bindi*—a red dot of *kumkum* and sandalwood—to their foreheads, throw a few grains of rice over them, and offer a special sweet in their honor.

vastu shanti ritual

The principal Hindu ritual associated with a new home is the *Vastu Shanti*, the invocation of the blessings of the celestial elements. Benevolent forces that rule the heavens are invited into the home and honored with worship and symbolic food, and offerings of flowers and festive fare are made to the *Vastu Purusha*, the Hindu deity that oversees all homes.

Color is everywhere. A courtyard is decorated with *rangoli* in honor of the festive season (above). Fine white powder is carefully drizzled through the fingers to outline robust, vivid designs. Here, a flurry of multi-colored parrots vie for honeyed blossoms in a traditional "tree-of-life" pattern.

regional styles

Each region of India has a definitive style that is echoed throughout the aesthetics of its homes. Kerala, on the southwestern coast, is known for its wooden houses, which delight in strong lines with few flourishes. In Kashmir, Himalayan flora inspires delicate embroidered shapes mimicking the leaves of the *chinar* tree—flowers and fruit designs appear in embroidery, carving, and moldings, and embellish homes and houseboats of the state.

a broad spectrum

Until recently, Indian style was considered by many foreigners to be synonymous with Rajasthan, the northern desert state famous for its bright colors. However, north Indian style also has a delicacy that is embodied in cities like Lucknow and Benares, where homes reflect an understated pride and orderliness and where cool white curtains and smooth marble walls are more likely to feature.

In Calcutta, Bombay (Mumbai), and Madras (Chennai), colonial buildings abound, yet each city has its own identity. Bombay is the biggest melting pot, the city of a million opportunities and the heart of India's movie industry, or "Bollywood." Here, homes reflect influences from the entire subcontinent as well as abroad and a variety of architectural styles are in evidence, from Islamic to Art Nouveau and Art Deco. In Calcutta and Madras, folk crafts from the region have amalgamated with urban sensibilities to create an aesthetic that enfolds European style with Indian rural and city tastes.

cultural influences

Indian style has also been influenced by the influx of cultures over many centuries. The Muslim influence is evident in the arches, domes, and ornate filigrees seen throughout north India, where the Mughals ruled for over four centuries. Then came the Europeans: first the Portuguese, who came in search of spices in 1497 and colonized Goa, Daman, and Diu; then the Dutch in 1595; and finally the British, who established their East India Company on the last day of 1600. Nineteenth-century colonial influence brought a love of both the Gothic and the baroque. As a result, it is not surprising to find a stiff Victorian edifice studded with gargoyles beside an ancient Hindu temple sculpted with sensuous gods.

Indian lifestyle also changed following colonization as Indians began to adopt some European tastes. Dining shifted from the floor to the table, and new types of furniture from coffee tables to hat stands began to appear in Indian homes.

heat and dust

The style and construction of homes that characterize the different regions of India are also influenced by climate and geography. In parts of Gujarat the sun is so fierce that mud is a popular material for walls, as it keeps interiors cool and pleasant. Brightly colored and patterned fabrics serve as doors, allowing gentle, intermittent breezes to waft through from the arid, treeless landscapes.

In coastal Goa, where the sea, the sand, and a sunny climate encourage a languid pace of life, verandas and patios are a defining part of the architecture, designed and built to catch the welcome breezes and to encourage much family activity to take place outside.

Vibrant color is everywhere in India (previous pages). From the intense hues worn by a traveling Sikh, through temple, palace, and domestic architecture.

Clean swathes of cotton dry in the bright Rajasthani sun at the Anokhi printing firm (left). Anokhi, a company run by Faith Singh, upholds the old traditions of Indian block-printed cloth.

earth, rain, and rivers were truly venerated and the destructive energy of primeval storms and earthquakes held people in awe.

In common with these beliefs, ancient sciences such as *ayurveda* (traditional Indian medicine) and *Vastu Shastra* (the science of construction and decorating) were directly or subtly linked with nature. Buildings and homes were built to balance the elements observed in nature, to encourage the flow of positive energy and thereby assure domestic health, wealth, and happiness. As Indians happily embrace the cycle that links humankind with nature and the universe, *Vastu Shastra* is still influential today and the five elements are widely celebrated in the decorative schemes of many Indian homes.

The sun's fiery orb, the rich earth, and the cool personality of water embody the greatness of the elements (above and right). A geometric form adopted by the Mughal conquerors in the sixteenthth century for their water filtration is shown (far right).

the five elements

The concept of the "five elements" (air, water, fire, earth, and space) has been woven into the fabric of India since before the arrival of the Aryans around 1500 B.C. Indian beliefs have always been animist—dedicated to the worship of nature. Although ancient Western beliefs recognize the first four elements, the fifth—space—is a more abstract principle. To many Indians, the notion of space represents the vast vacuum beyond ordinary perception and symbolizes the huge power of an unseen force. It is thus a source of inspiration in Hinduism and Zen Buddhism. The ancient animists worshipped trees and valued all plants, but the

and silver, is also ushered into Indian interiors by using materials that emphasize its qualities— long, light fabrics that dance in the summer breezes (as in the examples on page 153).

water—*jala*

Indians celebrate water (*jala*), symbolized by the color blue, in all its forms, from the oceans to the water of the humble well.

The Islamic invasion of A.D. 1200 led to the introduction of the *Char-bagh* (a mathematical plan of spiritual significance) to India. This plan represents a grid of waterways in which intersecting lines represent the four rivers of life and the interaction of God and man. A similar geometric form was adopted by the Mughal conquerors in the sixteenth century for their water filtration. This symbol appears in many parts of the country, from a private house in Rajasthan to the floor of a boutique in Bombay (as in the example on page 15).

fire—*agni*

One of the principal deities worshipped by the ancient Hindus was Agni, god of fire, and fire is still sacred today. Fire is symbolized by the colors red, orange, and gold. The most potent symbol of fire, the sun, is regarded as a special motif throughout India but especially in Gujarat, Rajasthan, and Orissa, where it embellishes furniture and fabric (as in the example on page 151).

earth—*bhoomi*

According to the *Vastu Shastra,* "Bhoomi Poojan"—earth worship—is necessary before any house construction begins.

Earthy colors and textures are very prominent

According to the *Vastu Shastra,* a home must be airy so that it can promote health and harmony. Billowing curtains (above) speak of gentle tropical breezes that ripple across an inviting planter's chair.

air—*vayu*

The *Vastu Shastra* emphasizes the importance of fresh air (*vayu*) in homes and buildings. The rooms in a home, the ancient text advises, must have efficient air circulation to ensure good health for the inhabitants. Because most of India is intensely hot, people try to circulate as much cool air through their home as they possibly can, be it with air conditioning, fans, or ventilators. Some old homes still have the remnants of the hand-drawn *"punkhas,"* which servants (*punkha-wallahs*) would operate. The element of air, often symbolized by white

in Indian homes and are used to stain floors, walls, furniture, and fabric, sometimes to create a backdrop for painted images. In the hottest regions, huts are made out of mud to keep the blistering heat at bay, and objects crafted out of clay abound in homes throughout the country (as in the example on page 52).

space—*akash*
In India, the vast landscape stretches beyond the realm of the naked eye. Yet in the cities, houses are small and clustered together and, in a land where social structures are based on the extended family, the Western concepts of personal space and privacy are irrelevant. So most rooms, even bedrooms, are communal. It is the allocation of space that is more important to Indians.

The expansion of the visual space is an art that has been well developed by Indian architects for hundreds of years. Walls are quite commonly punctuated with small windows, niches, and simple doorways. Open arches and filigreed screens between rooms demarcate areas that do not demand privacy (as in the example on page 132).

A solitary room suspended between two open vistas almost becomes a part of the endless space around it (above). Glass walls trick the eye into believing that the room is larger than it is.

living
spaces

space for **relaxation**

home and heart

Few Indians entertain the Western notion of a separate room for dining. In most modern Indian homes in towns and cities, the living room is also used as a room in which to eat. A complete set of seating furniture is a Western concept; many Indian people prefer a floor-level seating arrangement called a *baithak*. This comprises a thick, soft mattress that is placed against a wall to support the sitter's back, covered with a decorative fabric and scattered with cushions of different shapes, colors, and sizes that are either embroidered, mirror-worked, painted, or encrusted with tiny sequins.

Antique wood adds character to many Indian homes. A dramatic, curved plinth laid on an old tiled floor supports a *baithak* (main picture), and a church altar made into a mirror (above) reflects a Goan wood and cane *divan*.

complementary furniture

Collections of photographs, vases, boxes, and statues are sometimes arranged on *chowkies* or *piris* (low, four-legged wooden stools) that are as decorative as their displays. *Chowkies* are also used as seats to complement the floor-level *baithak* seating, or as foot-rests. Some *chowkies* have a straight or sloping high back that is carved or painted; these are often used as a *Dev-ghar* (altar for worship), to provide a beautiful background for three-dimensional images of gods and goddesses.

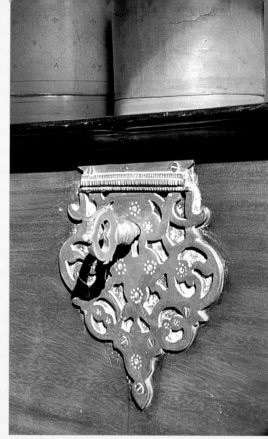

The colors of an Indian summer are captured in this elegant room. One side is a perpetual invitation to a game of *shatranj* (chess), the other a perfect place to relax amidst a row of polished brass vessels and a colorful quilt on the wall. Looking on in silence is a 300-year-old wooden Maharashtrian statue.

quiltmaker's mansion, bombay

Geeta Khandelwal, an award-winning quilt and patchwork artist, lives in an ancestral home in a sought-after and leafy area of Bombay. Behind the unassuming gates of her property lies a jewel of a mansion, built in stages between 1898 and 1962, and now almost completely obscured by flowering trees that are constantly full of the sound of happy songbirds.

The main door to the private apartments opens to reveal a succession of arches and windows. An old wrought-iron balcony with a green mosaic-floored terrace leads off from the drawing room.

A grand *divan*, more than sixty years old and of colonial Goan design, crafted out of curved wood and woven cane, dominates the drawing room. It is perfectly placed to catch the cool breezes that waft through the tropical garden outside.

Light and shade create a kaleidoscope of special effects on a beaten brass table from Rajasthan (left), where a pair of elephant bells stands guard over a collection of iron scissors that were used for cutting cloth during the 18th century. Standing proudly against an orange wall is a wooden horse carriage—an antique that was used as a toy in the 18th century. On another low table (above) is a wicker and brass basket and a profusion of wild sunflowers that match the bright yellow wall. The entrance to this room (right) is decorated with a Gujarati mirror and cowrie-shell *toran* (bunting) and beyond, a latticed door-frame mounted on the wall creates an illusion of a Mughal window.

The universal appeal of book-lined shelves and a grandfather clock is given a peculiarly Indian touch with the addition of a Rajasthani puppet doll and a wooden sentinel, or *dwar-pal,* which holds the door ajar.

swing chairs

Heavy and ornate, swing chairs have a special significance in the folklore of India. Gods and goddesses are said to swing ambivalently in soft flowering bowers and young maidens await their lovers on swings in cool emerald glades. The swing, variously called the *jhoola*, *hindola*, or *zhopala*, is also used in rituals. Hindus often place their deities on decorative swings, as the to-and-fro movement is supposed to signify a state of bliss and create a sense of detachment from the cares of the mortal world. The continuous, monotonous swinging movement is believed to elevate and introduce one to a divine energy.

Swing style varies according to its state of origin. Gujarat and Rajasthan have especially beautiful ones, from the exquisite pure silver filigreed styles to the more affordable painted wooden ones. A typical example of a Gujarati swing is the wooden *sankheda* on which well-loved motifs such as parrots, mangoes, and flowers are painted in blazing orange on a glossy black, red, or vibrant green lacquered backdrop. The swing can also be embellished with wooden tassels and bells that make a delightful sound as it rocks back and forth.

Richly carved swings from the south are too large and heavy for anything but gentle, lazy movements. Influenced by temple carvings, they are decorated with motifs such as caparisoned elephants, bells, and amazingly voluptuous images of deities.

In the modern home, bold, fearless color can create a beautiful contrast between piles of soft cushions and the stark geometric lines of the swing.

Aman Nath and Francis Wacziarg, known for their skill in restoring heritage properties, have created a restful spot at Neemrana Fort Palace (above) and at their private retreat, Fawn Haveli, near Delhi (right).

A giant Nataraja presides over this formal sitting room (left), located in the center of the house. The fiery wood tones are tempered by a soft light from above, which filters through an airy white Jamdani fabric. Niches display miniature paintings; an assortment of polished brass vessels cluster on a central table; and a classical statue makes a clever lamp base.

beautiful homes

Ahmedabad in Gujarat has some of the most beautiful homes in the country. In one such house, a wooden porch ushers visitors into the living room, where the seating is in the form of a swing, shieldback chairs, and a carved bench inlaid with old floral tiles. The color and working of the wood are accented by deep red, mirrorwork floor cushions, which are grouped around a low, square, centrally placed table.

The swing in this home is flanked by tall pillars, square and round, that are completely engulfed by detailed carving. Etched glass lamps in pink and blue tints recall an old world ambience, and swathes of embroidered fabric and brass parrots make a lively mobile at the entrance to an adjoining room.

Features like the family of wooden statues (top left), the eclectic assortment of cushions (top), and the burnished metalware (left) add to the swirl of color, pattern, and texture in both these rooms.

A cool vanilla room at Neemrana Fort Palace, punctuated by niches and a big flower-shaped arch. The leaf-patterned fabric is repeated in a quiet writing corner (left) and in the main *baithak* (right), which follows a traditional seating plan seen at concerts of classical music, where connoisseurs recline on bolsters as they enjoy their favorite *raga,* or melody.

rajasthani palatial style

Rajasthan, in the north of India, is home to innumerable palaces, both large and small. The most sumptuous of these are a mix of colonial opulence (Italian marble and stained glass windows) and Indian ornamentation (gilded walls and ceilings, and gold filigreed screens). Lapis and onyx Rajput miniatures decorate bedroom walls and crystal chandeliers, and shining colored glass balls hang down in the spacious drawing rooms.

divans

Another piece of seating furniture commonly encountered is a low wooden bedstead called a *divan*. The use of *divans* has now spread far beyond the subcontinent. Some of the most appealing *divans* have beautifully carved legs and panels.

Old colonial *divans* were used to rest on during the heat of the day and occasionally at night. Some have a beautiful, lacelike belt of fine woven cane running down their center line, reminiscent of the decoration of the furniture in the old houses of the tea plantations and the hill stations.

private commissions

Wooden furniture plays a major part in most Indian interiors, and as skilled carpenters have always been happy to work to specific patterns, many people in India commission pieces of their own design. Not only does this prove to be the cheapest practice, but it has had the effect of encouraging many hybrid Indian styles to flourish. Indian craftsmen fashion timber to make elegant, durable furniture, ranging from radiant gold pine to the rich brown of teak, which lends color and warmth to the decor.

craftsmanship

One of the most famous sources of wooden furniture is Saharanpur, near Delhi. The craftsmen here are predominantly Muslim, and Mughal influences such as tiny cusped arches, lush floral fretwork, and fluted minarets abound in their work. Heavy, distinctive sheshamwood sofas, chairs, and tables made in Saharanpur can be seen all over India.

Blue finds expression at Nilaya Hermitage (left). Nilaya (which means blue sky) is a small designer hotel in Goa where organic motifs and artifacts lend each room a unique atmosphere. The monsoon color also makes an effective backdrop (above) to plump piled cushions and a mélange of framed shoes.

In Delhi itself, craftsmen are particularly adept at making a special kind of furniture in which tiny, delicately carved pieces of ivory seem to be woven through their designs. These days, as people have become aware of the endangered status of the elephant, ivory has been replaced by other materials such as creamy chips of stone or plaster, which are just as effective.

In Gujarat, some living rooms feature decorated pillars of dark wood. These not only support the structure of the house but contribute to the aesthetic appeal of the room. Little, detailed motifs such as parrots, flowers, and peacocks are painted in vibrant primary colors, or the entire column is given a wash of dull gold.

goan tilework

Most Indian tabletops are beautifully handcrafted. Tables inspired by Parsee, Indo-Iranian, and colonial Goan influences have tops and sides finished with old floral tiles in jeweled colors, a style that is becoming increasingly popular. Goa abounds in tables decorated with *azulejos*, decorative tiles that still carry their Portuguese name. These tables also have the

Rosa Costa Dias lives in this 19th-century ancestral mansion in Goa, decorated in a mix of Portuguese, Chinese, Indian, and European styles. The Regency-style sofa (left) catches a tropical sunbeam, while the fresh lime color of the arched Gothic door (right) ensures that the cool interior of the house remains calm and restful.

The Nrityagram dance village near Bangalore is where all forms of Indian classical dance are taught by *gurus.* Designed by Gerard da Cunha to satisfy every dancer's need to feel the earth under her feet and the sky on her skin, this *gurukul,* or school, is a study in stone, mud, and brick. All kinds of natural textures touched with an incandescent gold beg to be caressed even as the seating, almost a continuation of the earth itself, provides a respite from the rigors of classical training.

trademark *torcidos e tremidos* (meaning turned and twisted) legs. This Iberian style became popular in Portugal during the Spanish occupation of 1500–1640 and as a result found its way to the former Portuguese colony of Goa. Contemporary designers draw on the Iberian theme to create tables, chairs, and consoles with custom-made tiles in complementary or monochromatic color schemes.

northern inlay

The Taj Mahal at Agra, built by the Mughal emperor Shah Jahan for his beloved wife Mumtaz Mahal, has inspired innumerable patterns for elegant furniture made in the north: pink lilies in rose quartz with sage-green jade leaves embellish smooth marble tops, and fruit-colored precious and semi-precious gems such as lapis lazuli, agate, turquoise, bloodstone, and red cornelian are inlaid in fine mother-of-pearl veneers to create rich, swirling designs and tones.

brasswork

Moradabad in the state of Uttar Pradesh produces tabletops made from beaten brass; in the south too, brass tables and low stools add a gleam to more muted wood and terra-cotta interiors.

pottery

India has its own version of the characteristic blue and white pottery from Delft. Jaipur, in Rajasthan, produces exquisite ceramics: urns, jars, fruit bowls, and countless other functional and decorative objects in cerulean shades that range from cobalt to sapphire and cyan. Earthy Khurja pottery from Uttar Pradesh is chunkier

and more rustic, but it is bright, inexpensive, and readily available; it also highlights the use of black, rust, and green in color schemes. Khurja is close to the Mughal-influenced regions of India, so many objects crafted in the region—such as the *surahi* (a long, tall jug)—are inspired by Islamic design.

hill station style

A rare but beautiful feature seen in some drawing rooms—especially in north India, which has very cold winters—is a fireplace. The ones that remain in some old traditional or colonial homes are typically British in style. Jubbal Palace, set on a mountainside near Simla, is a masterpiece of Victorian, Gothic, Art Deco, and local architecture. The focus of the formal dining room is a heavy paneled and carved wooden fireplace. Above this hangs an unsurpassed collection of miniature paintings from Himachal Pradesh, which reflect the cool, verdant surroundings of this mountainous region. Heavy carpets and draperies also add much needed warmth.

eclectic display

Beautiful objects and interesting artifacts are often passed down from one generation to the next; it is therefore not unusual to see a beautiful bronze statue of Nataraja, the Lord of Dance, from southern India, sitting beside a Rajasthani *pichwai* (painted hanging cloth) of Radha and Krishna at play amongst colorful peacocks and lotuses. A mixture of brass trays, bowls, and pots crafted to resemble fine lace or beaten to create relief patterns sits next to jewel-toned glassware; these will usually be from the state of Uttar Pradesh. Silver filigreed objects

Tropical fruit, vibrant plants, and a luminous sculpture of translucent leaves designed by Priti Paul add zest to her modern Delhi apartment (left). In the bedroom, a solitary contemporary chair (above) meditates upon a painting of fighting cocks by the Tamil artist and designer Thota Tharani.

from Gujarat, Orissa, and Rajasthan, such as photograph frames, jugs, and vases, can add a simple elegance. Wooden mythical beasts from Gujarat silently guard doorways and classical bronze statues of gods and goddesses in the *Chola* style of south India—typified by long, lean headgear and perfect facial features—fit into illuminated alcoves. Garments made from ancient and precious fabrics like the old *patolas* from Orissa and Andhra Pradesh are often preserved as wall hangings.

motifs

Certain motifs that have special meaning reoccur in furniture and artifacts. The lotus takes pride of place and has always stood for beauty, sanctity, divinity, and detachment from such worldly distractions as greed, anger, and jealousy. This essentially Hindu, Buddhist, and Jain motif is a universal symbol because the lotus produces perfect beauty from the unlikely sustenance of brackish pools.

Another image popularly seen on fabrics and furniture is that of a celestial couple making love. In Hindu art the couple, or *mithuna*, signifies the cosmic union of man and god, which goes beyond the physical. All Hindus understand the four principles of *dharma* (duty), *artha* (earning wealth), *moksha* (salvation), and *kama* (sexual love), and Indian art has no qualms about displaying scenes of procreation and sexual ecstasy.

space for entertainment

Indians love music. Musical instruments are revered as bearers of knowledge and are treated with the same respect as gods. A *sitar*, *tanpura,* or pair of *tablas* will have their own special corner where they are out of the way—contact by human foot signifies disrespect and carelessness. Many musically oriented families bring out the instruments after dinner and enjoy each other's company in informal concerts that are full of mutual admiration and jollity. Some families even arrange informal musical gatherings and invite professional or semi-professional artists to perform for a select audience.

Other hobbies that are pursued in this room include indoor games. Here, cards are at the top of the list. Traditional games such as *shatranj*, or chess—played with cowrie shells—are also popular in some parts of the country.

A family-owned Chettinad house in Madras, enriched with jewel-like Indian craftsmanship: Tanjore glass paintings, stained glass (left), and a collection of vibrant glass bottles from Uttar Pradesh that catch the rays of the morning sun (right).

Luz House, built in 1850, stands in the heart of Madras. Decorated by two Frenchmen, Jean François Lesage and Patrick Savouret, the salon downstairs (right) is dominated by painted columns and bright cobalt walls, which reflect the neoclassical architecture and the colors of a huge portrait of a former owner.

Four steps (left) annex a little sitting room to the wooden pavilion that sits on the roof of the house to catch the sea breezes. Every room is filled with an eclectic mix of Indian and European artifacts, such as the lamp shaded with finely hand-painted leather from Andhra Pradesh (above), which softly lights a Lesage cushion cover design.

Art Deco–style chair (left), harking back to the boom of the 1930s, when the new style took root and fast replaced the fashion for the Victorian influence such as the cast-iron garden seat, originally c.1860 (far left).

Planter's chairs (left) are now found throughout India. They are indicative of European colonial influence. They were designed so that the weary plantation owner could stretch his legs out on the arms of his chair as he rested on the veranda with his gin and tonic.

The consummate skills of Indian artisans and craftsmen allow them to turn their hand to any style. This wrought-iron chair (right) was commissioned to complement Dean D'Cruz's bold interior designs at Nilaya Hermitage in Goa.

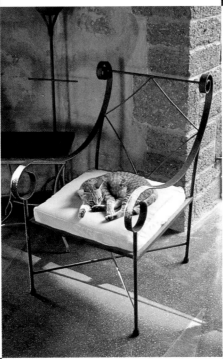

The Dutch first settled in India in the 1500s, and brought their own stylistic influences and designs. India, in typical magpie fashion, synthesized these readily. This chair (right) is based upon a 20th-century (Rietveld) cubist idea.

Old colonial homes in India still have heavy and robust cane or bamboo furniture (left), which puts to rest the notion that such furniture is only for occasional use. This modern piece is typical of furniture made for export to Europe and America.

Another popular seat is the swing (left), variously called the *jhoola*, *hindola*, or *zhopala*. It is often used in Hindu rituals, as the to-and-fro movement is said to signify a state of bliss and detachment from the everyday cares of the mortal world.

family worship

In almost every country in the world, a home has a central focus where the family gathers. In Western countries this focus was often the fireplace; in India it was the place of worship. Once upon a time, this was where the household would pay obeisance to the god of their choice in peaceful and quiet surroundings. Much later, after Hindu temples and Buddhist *viharas* had been built, congregational worship began, but the tradition of home worship continued and still remains strong. Some form of worship still brings the household together at particular times.

This area of worship is more often than not in the kitchen. A mini temple called a *mandir* for Hindus, an altar for Christians, and a prayer mat for Muslims are all given a special sanctified area that is kept scrupulously clean. Hindus and Christians take great pleasure in decorating their temple or altar with garlands of flowers and other symbolic elements as well as extremely beautiful works of art, often handmade in the home. Many old Goan colonial homes have Gothic altars resplendent with gold and enamel detail and containing a fantastic host of Catholic artifacts such as votive candles and images of the sacred heart. Many Hindu homes have a separate room called the *pooja* (worship) room where the images of various deities are revered. This room is kept fragrant with incense and a little oil lamp burns throughout the day and night. The family gathers in the *pooja* room each morning or evening to offer worship and sing devotional hymns.

space for eating

food and ritual

Terra-cotta pots, used in
villages to store and
keep water cool, make a
delightful display in the
home (overleaf), and a
row of colorful spices
lines every kitchen shelf.

India's most modern, gleaming kitchens are a
far cry from the traditional ones of the past,
where decoration was limited to simple
drawings of motifs representing plenitude and
prosperity. The *kumbha,* or pot, is one such
motif; in Hindu mythology, when the great

oceans were churned by the gods and the
demons in their search for the nectar of
immortality, it was Dhanvantari, the doctor of
the gods, who arose from the frothy waters
holding the legendary *kumbha* full of nectar.
The *kumbha* symbolizes good luck, and when
first entering a new home, the head of a Hindu
family will carry a *kumbha* decorated with a
coconut and fresh mango leaves.

Like the *kumbha*, the coconut is another popular symbol used to decorate Indian kitchens. Called *shriphal*, meaning the fruit of the gods, it is revered for its multiple uses. The coconut features in ritual worship and sometimes takes the place of deities when it is ceremonially anointed with fragrant sandalwood paste and decorated with flowers. The mango is also a source of inspiration for kitchen decor. This national fruit of India is greatly loved and can be found represented in paisley-type patterns, used as decorations on walls and floors.

simple vessels

So entrenched in Indian life is the humble pot that every kitchen has a smooth, terra-cotta vessel in which to keep water cool. The pot also imbues the water with a delicate, earthy fragrance; many people prefer this naturally cooled water to water chilled in the refrigerator. In fact, in some regions where the climate is dry and hot, hard-working vendors carry these *matkas,* or earthen pots, full of cold water on bicycles and sell it by the cup to thirsty, grateful travellers.

On the whole, Indian kitchens are rather stark, simple rooms with little decoration. This is because at heart they are utilitarian rooms meant for the family, close relatives, and friends. Entertaining never takes place here and objects are chosen and placed for their function rather than their aesthetic appeal. Commonly seen are rows of gleaming gold- and silver-colored storage boxes made of steel or brass and containing cereals, lentils, and flours, as well as savory and sweet snacks for tea.

At the heart of every Indian housewife's kitchen—village or city, poor or wealthy—is her spice box. This can be a simple, practical wooden box, or a more ornate filigreed silver or brass example— itself a work of art. Inside the spice box are small compartments and individual spoons for all the main spices used in the cooking. Occasionally antique spice boxes turn up in old shops or flea markets and these can be astonishingly beautiful.

Also used to store spices are glass jars that highlight the vibrant colors of the contents, such as madder-red chili powder, saffron-hued turmeric, sage-colored cumin, and parrot-green fennel seeds, adding drama to this otherwise functional room.

simple versus chic

Rustic kitchens are brightened with strings of garlic and all kinds of onions, from pearly white to glossy pink and purple, suspended from the ceiling. Bottle green to blazing orange pumpkins of every shape and size are hung in rope nets for use when out of season. Herbs are used fresh and the window sill is

Only the spices and a small terra-cotta horse suggest the Indianness of this contemporary kitchen, where a wooden *jali* separates the space (left). The relief on the living area wall (above) gives a similar clue.

lined with little pots containing mint, coriander, lemongrass, and basil.

The various spice mixtures and pastes demand an efficient grinding system; traditionally, a grinding stone with a flat plinth was used to reduce herbs, spices, and vegetables to a fine purée. These days, state-of-the-art blenders are used in many urban kitchens. Long cooking procedures are made simple by the use of pressure cookers, and by mid-morning the sounds emanating from the kitchen include the hiss of spices hitting the oil, the whistle of the pressure cooker, and the dull whirring of the blender concocting aromatic mixes.

In the villages, water is stored in large vats. These can be extremely ornate, and have found admirers in wealthier Indian homes, where they have been adopted as decorative urns or vases. They can be painted or embossed with plaster of Paris, encrusted with sequins, beads, or tiny chips of mirror, or made even more vibrant with the application of gold or silver fabric.

the god of fire

The element of fire is considered sacred by the Hindus and Parsees. As the fire in any house is contained in the kitchen, according to *Vastu Shastra* this room is governed by the god of fire, Agnidev. In the *Vastu* chart specifying the location of the various rooms in a home, it is recommended that the kitchen be located in the southeast, as this is the direction ruled by Agni. Furthermore, the cook should always face the east while cooking, a practice probably encouraged to make maximum use of available light at sunrise, when most of the day's cooking would be done. The water source, according to the *Vastu Shastra*, should be in the northeast

Different styles: Indo-Portuguese colonial style (left), organic (below left), contemporary (above), and Raj influence (right)—all create a convivial atmosphere for good food, soothing music, and exciting conversation.

corner, and for safety, shelves and storage space should be built on the south or west side, away from the fire. In addition, the rigorous heat and overpoweringly fragrant ingredients that Indian cooking involves mean that the kitchen must be well-ventilated.

old traditions

In traditional India, segregation of men and women is still the norm. On social occasions, the women gather in the kitchen and lend a hand in preparing and serving the meal. They rarely eat with the men, unless the family is particularly Westernized.

indian hospitality

Entertaining guests with good food, soothing music, and vibrant conversation is at the heart of Indian hospitality. Hosts and guests often sit on the floor to eat, as they have done for centuries. For everyday use, the typical Indian plate, bowl, and other vessels are made of stainless steel; on special occasions brass or silver is used. Of course, many people these days also use cutlery, but most Indians claim that the best way to enjoy the textures of Indian food is to eat with the fingers.

The serving of food is an art in itself. Utensils used for cooking and serving are made of stainless steel, brass, or copper. Some conservative families keep separate utensils for serving vegetarian and nonvegetarian food; Hindus have a mostly vegetarian diet while Muslims and Sikhs are bigger meat-eaters. *Kadais,* also called *karahis* (Indian "woks"), made of iron or aluminum are often hung along the wall as a form of decor.

space for **sleeping**

bedrooms

All bedrooms must be comfortable, and in India this primarily means cool, so every Indian house has an assortment of fans on tables, pedestals, and ceilings. A whirring fan is often the only movement in the stillness of a dense, hot afternoon or long summer night, when the eagerly-awaited dawn arrives on the wings of songbirds. Nights are permeated by a lazy heat but mornings are fresh and peaceful with a latent, expectant energy.

It is reassuring to awake to see something dear to the heart, and many traditional Hindus hang an image of their favorite deity on the wall opposite the bed so that it is the first thing they see in the morning. The bedroom is also used to display favorite objects like statuettes, colored glass bottles and bowls, carved or enameled boxes, and paintings depicting scenes from the epics.

Diffused lighting, straightforward color schemes, and simple motifs make these bedrooms neat and elegant.

In contrast, the elaborate room of the previous pages is actually an old hunting tent where bird and animal prints imitate the wildlife outside. At night, when the lamps are turned off, guests fall asleep lulled by the sound of the tent sides gently flapping in the breeze.

A white canopy (left),
diaphanous curtains (above),
and a white mosquito net
(right) serve to keep
airborne pests at bay while
creating a romantic ambience
in each of these well lit
bedrooms, where the
judicious use of aqua blue
adds to the impression of
cool and calm.

the right position

According to the *Vastu Shastra*, it is not lucky to use a broken bed or to place a bed in the extreme corners of a room. The sensible reasoning behind this is that in an emergency, there should be enough space around the bed to allow a quick escape. For the same reason, the bed should not touch any walls of the room, says the ancient text. And it should be placed so that the person's head points to the south. This is because the *Vastu Shastra* believes the body acts like a magnet. Therefore, if the head (as the heaviest and most important part) were towards the north, it would repel against the north pole of the earth, adversely affecting blood circulation. This, says the *Vastu Shastra,* will result in tension and disturbed sleep.

the role of the bedroom

Today, the Indian bedroom serves many purposes, but in a traditional society where men and women often socialize separately, it is here that the women often retreat to talk and gossip.

In India, great importance is placed on the bedroom in terms of use and decoration. The Indian family system places a major share of the child-rearing responsibility on the grandparents, so it is common for them to sleep in the same

Mirrors that deflect the evil eye and protect the unassuming sleeper watch vigilantly over these beds. Both the mirrors are set into wooden frames, lush with flowers and foliage, that serve as a point of focus in these rooms which are rich in color, pattern, and architectural detail.

A painting of the goddess Saraswati first greets the sleeper's eye on waking in this sunny bed.

A collection of handmade boxes and artifacts purchased from some of India's countless markets.

There is a hint of pattern and color that embellishes the ivory simplicity of this romantic canopied bed.

Floating heads of brazenly colored flowers are used as a bold form of decoration all over India.

nuptial preparation

The bedroom is specially decorated during weddings for the nuptial night. Women of the family hang long chains of tiny, fragrant flowers around the room and over the bed, which is also strewn with rose petals. Glasses of saffron-flavored milk, considered an aphrodisiac, are placed discreetly beside the bed after the wedding and before the wedding night. The bride, bedecked with jewels and silks, waits for the groom in this room. In traditional arranged marriages, this is where they meet alone for the very first time.

functional to the sublime

Many specialists in India believe that the *charpoy*, which is a kind of low bed (the word means "four legs"), was the first piece of formal furniture to be made. Early Indian bed designs

According to *Vastu Shastra*, the bedroom is governed by Agni, the god of fire, which includes sexual fires. His color, red, adds a patina of passion to many bedrooms in India (left). A carved chair matches a column topped with *yakshis*, or heavenly maidens (below left), creating a make-believe atrium within the room. A cotton printed curtain parts tantalizingly (right) to reveal a bed with posts that gleam in the soft incandescence.

room as the children. However, young married couples always have a bedroom of their own. The Hindu faith acknowledges the importance of the act of consummation: sex is not taboo in Indian art and literature, and treatises like the *Kama Sutra* describe intimate details of the act without any qualms.

rural practices

Some rural communities, like the Bannis of Kutch in Gujarat, live in a single circular room and their sleeping arrangements are simple to assemble and dismantle. They will sleep on mattresses, unfurled at night and rolled up and stacked in one corner during the day. Colorful handcrafted patchwork quilts are draped over the bedding to add a spot of brightness to an otherwise frugal home.

had feet resembling the sharp-clawed paws of animals and were richly decorated with silk bedspreads and frills. Four round, decorative cushions in contrasting colors would be placed at the four corners for effect. Beds were large and heavy and generally occupied the center of a room.

Today, different parts of India produce different kinds of beds. The poorest people use a simple *khatiya,* a rough bed made of four wooden legs held together by a thick net of coir rope. Slightly more comfortable is the *charpoy,* or low wooden bedstead. These are fairly portable, so in areas where summers can get unbearably hot, people take advantage of the flat terraces on top of their homes and convert them into communal bedrooms at night. There the men will sit talking and smoking as breezes usher in the moonlit night. Although somewhat plain, the *charpoy* can be made into a feature by dressing it with bright fabric and cushions.

maharaja's fantasy

In a country that has given us the *Kama Sutra,* it is natural that some beds were designed purely to promote sexual pleasure. Swing beds, beds that floated in lotus pools, and beds that had tiny chambers in which to store fragrance and aphrodisiacs can be found in erotic Indian literature. A few Indian palaces, even today, have unusual beds that reflect the taste of their owners, the erstwhile maharajas. Some of them had a preference for hanging beds, suspended from the ceiling by thick chains. These days one rarely finds these floating beds—they remain only as relics of India's royal past. Similarly, the very high beds found in some grand palaces are increasingly difficult to find. Decorative steps, or

carved chests, were kept next to these huge beds, so that the royal person literally had to climb into bed.

wooden beds

Wooden beds from the southern states of Tamil Nadu and Kerala are especially famous for their chiseled beauty. In Kashmir, in the foothills of the Himalayas, houseboats on lily-festooned lakes attracted large numbers of honeymooning couples until political problems halted tourism. While visitor numbers have fallen, the expansive beds covering entire sides of the low, wide boats can still be found. Often framed within vanilla- and cream-colored cusped arches, they are decorated with gold and silver cushions, while a *surahi* (tall, slender jug) completes the opulent effect. These houseboats are the perfect retreat for lovers, the gently lapping water the only sound that disturbs the cool mountain air.

Rooms within rooms expand and unite space simultaneously. Here, a large bed fills an entire arched doorway (left) but still looks languorous, and a bed chamber (above) provides a delightful arena for the play of light and air.

The energy of many suns suffuses this organic bedroom in Goa (left). While simple lines and sweeping curves punctuate the continuous color, sunshine hues of peach, lemon, copper, and gold create radiance. Another bedroom in Goa (above) has a tranquil corner: a wood and cane rocking chair and an old Christian image of the blessed virgin set the mood for prayer and introspection.

air in. What's more, the posts provide ample scope for intricate wood carving.

In south India, Gujarat, and Uttar Pradesh, carved four-poster beds are made of dark wood and can lend an incredibly luxurious look to a bedroom. The posts are festooned with swags of bright cotton or satin material, while extra lengths are left to cascade down to the floor in a spectacular fashion.

India has many different kinds of four-poster beds, such as the slim bent metal one (left), festooned with lavender muslin, and the luxurious polished brass one (below). Simple yet elegant posts frame a painting of Krishna (near right), whereas the antique bed (far right) is a sumptuous confection in mirror, wood, and fabric.

decorated surfaces

Cane and wrought-iron, crafted in swirls and curls, also merge to create a typical Indian style of bed. The bases of cane beds are reinforced by the use of additional cane, bamboo, or rough coir matting to cope with everyday use. Sometimes a simple cane network is woven onto wooden frames—a structure that can be found in colonial-style, Goan furniture.

four posters

Four-poster beds universally conjure up visions of romance and excitement and they are popular all over India. They also have a practical use: Sleep can be disturbed by mosquitoes and other flying insects, but a four-poster bed will conveniently support a light mosquito net to keep the insects out while letting much wanted

children's bedrooms

Indian bedrooms for children, like bedrooms for children around the world, are full of colorful mobiles and pictures. The only difference is that the wonderfully multicolored parrots with bells on their feet, or quivering fish and peacocks with red and yellow tails suspended over cribs and cots in India are more likely to be made of wood, silk, and other attractive natural materials rather than lurid plastic.

Some of the most opulent children's rooms must also surely be found in India. As a baby, the Maharaja of Jodhpur was put into a luxurious silver cradle that was beautifully decorated with little models of sari-clad angels. The simple touch of an ingeniously placed button was all that was needed to start the gentle rocking movement of this cradle extraordinaire.

One of the finest examples of a four-poster bed can be found in the bedroom of a successful fisheries expert from Cochin. The bed takes pride of place in the center of the room and has been fashioned out of old, dark wood. Each post is carved with scenes from the Indian epic *Mahabharata,* and this masterpiece stands an impressive three feet high. The other furniture in the bedroom fades against the red and black tribal-print cotton swags and cushions that add drama to an already spectacular piece.

In an old, colonial home in Goa there is another impressive four-poster bed, embellished with mirror panels and inlaid with colored tiles. The bed is given a romantic touch by being covered with a simple, white crocheted bedspread. A matching console and dresser intensify the quiet charm.

dressing up

Indian folklore and mythology are full of doe-eyed, creamy-skinned heroines who spend hours at their *toilette* preparing to receive handsome lovers. The image of a beautiful woman gazing admiringly and expectantly into a mirror is one that is repeated endlessly in Indian temple and domestic decoration and enforces every woman's right to admire herself.

The dressing table is every woman's personal retreat, where she stores the secret potions and mixtures that enhance or maintain her looks. This piece of furniture can be made of richly carved wood featuring motifs like the large, shady, and luscious *kalpavriksha,* or the tree of life, or motifs of elephants, flowers, or fruits, which are all greatly cherished.

Three traditional beauties gaze through a series of arched doorways that are inspired by Islamic design and that contribute an antique aesthetic to this modern bedroom (far left). Chairs upholstered in scarlet raw silk provide the ideal reading corner and cool marble flooring affirms that the home is in a hotter part of the country. Colonial Britain still lives on in many Indian homes (left), and old and new, traditional and foreign elements are all brought together in a daring palette of color (above).

sola singaar

Dressing tables can also be made of cane, metal, or clay and used to store other bedroom necessities. Personal care is especially important in Hindu culture, which has for centuries expected women to be beautifully presented at all times. Ancient Sanskrit literature laid down the concept of *Sola Singaar,* sixteen traditional ornamentations with which any woman can beautify herself. These accoutrements are for every Hindu woman, irrespective of class, and they can be made of precious gems, wood, glass, or even fragrant, colorful flowers. The sixteen adornments comprise the *bindi,* the dot worn on the forehead; necklaces and garlands; earrings; flowers in the hair; bangles; rings; armlets worn on the upper arm; waistbands or belts; anklets for the feet; toe-rings; *kohl* (black eyeliner) for the eyes; henna for the hands and feet; perfume; sandalwood paste to polish and perfume the body; the upper garment; and, lastly, the lower garment.

wedding gifts

It is customary in some communities for parents to give their daughter a cupboard with a safe as part of her wedding trousseau. These are often richly carved with motifs including grapevines, flowers, fruits, and trees. In south India, traditional symbols like

Velvet cushions, a luxurious rug (used as a throw), and a painted tasseled canopy (left) present a tongue-in-cheek pastiche of royal residential style. The blue and white patterns of the furnishings in this room (above) are a celebration of traditional Indian block-printed textile designs.

the conch or the peacock are preferred.

In Kutch in Gujarat, tribal communities fashion storage units out of clay, which are then whitewashed and embellished with small irregular bits of mirror. These mirrors are believed to reflect all negative forces and therefore ward off the "evil eye."

superstitions

Some communities hang a string of chilies and a lemon on the handles of jewelry cupboards on festive days. Good fortune, either wealth or success, is considered to attract the evil eye in the form of envy and ill wishes, so people practice various traditional rituals to protect themselves.

In rural India, various motifs thought to encourage good luck are painted onto cupboards to safeguard the contents. The snake is popular, as in Indian mythology snakes are the guardians of secret and celestial treasures.

Bedroom decor can be versatile and changeable, as it is the bedroom that most reflects personal tastes, moods, and pursuits.

Many Indian bedrooms are painted bright white or pale, creamy vanilla to keep the heat at bay. Fantasy plays a great part here, and canopies, festoons, lamps, candles, and traditional decorative objects can all create an ethereal look. This is not a room in which fantasy should be limited.

space for **washing**

bathing

Bathrooms are rooms with no rules. Personal fancies and preferences reign supreme, and a sense of privacy and self indulgence are the only parameters along which they can be designed and decorated.

Since ancient times, Hindus have regarded bathing as a ritual to cleanse not only the physical body, but also as a process of cleansing the spiritual soul. According to the scriptures, this ritual bath, called *snana,* is best performed in flowing water—a river, spring, or waterfall. In the villages where nature, space, and communal living allow more liberty than in the more cramped cities, people still bathe in rivers and streams.

The ancient civilizations of Mohenjo–Daro and Harrappa had communal baths, with flights of steps or sloping banks to gently lower the worshipper from the material world into a transitional place where, symbolically, communication with a higher world was possible. This whole concept of purification has been passed down through the generations and is still practiced by Hindus today.

ceremonial bathing

The *Vastu Shastra* has much to say about the ideal location of a bathroom within a house. It should be in the east so as to catch the mild, cleansing rays of the morning sun and flood the bathing space with light, thus promoting health. This location is also appropriate for the Hindu practice of offering prayer to the rising sun soon after one's bath.

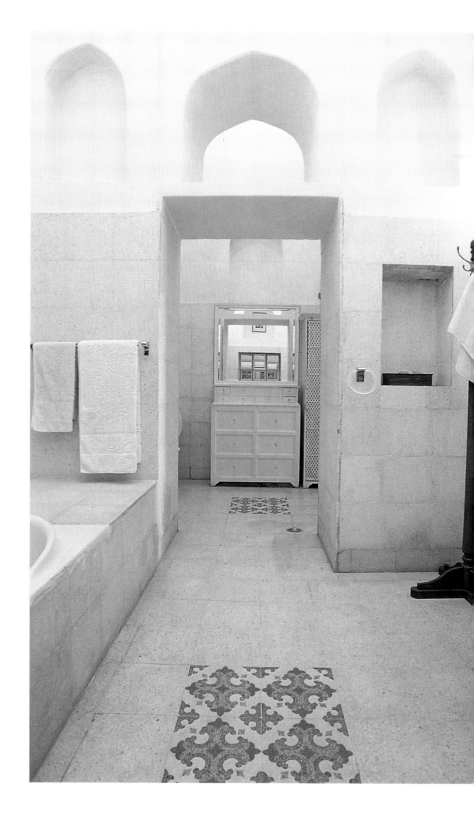

In India, a ceremonial bath is also given to deities before worshipping them. It is customary to bathe them in *panchamrita* or the traditional ambrosia made of a mixture of milk, *ghee* (clarified butter), yogurt, honey, and sugar. The holy statues are then washed down with water.

A Hindu bride is given a cleansing and purifying bath with turmeric and fresh cream after which she cannot leave her house until the time of the wedding. This ceremony is performed by the women of the household and is full of giggling innuendos and high spirits.

exotic practices

The concept of exotic bathing was really made into a fine art by the erstwhile Indian maharajas who had their gold and silver bathtubs filled with warm scented water and strewn with crimson rose petals.

Both bathrooms (previous spread) in the Nilaya Hermitage celebrate the natural elements through celestial motifs and organic architecture. Designer Dean D'Cruz uses china mosaic that gleams in the sunlight, while a fan-shaped mirror and a wall pierced with crosses allow the bather to look out into the gardens.

The sense of space in bathrooms is often accentuated with dramatic tiles that recall palace verandas (left and above right). Niches and arches curve sensuously into the wall and the rooms look almost too lavish for their simple function.

A spectacular display of tiles in flower and beast patterns (right) suggests limitless decorative possibilities.

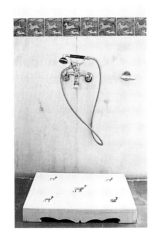

Today, India's most stylish bathrooms house an assortment of exotic fragrances, skin softeners, polishers, and nourishers. Many of these toiletries find their inspiration in old Indian texts that show images of queens and princesses sitting beside beautiful marble baths, their long tresses floating in the water, as hand-maidens anoint their bodies with beautifying herbs, creams, and potions. These majestic pools, dotted with blushing lotuses, were the meeting places and playgrounds for the royal women. Even today, Indian women indulge themselves with milk baths and herbal soaps, and exotic scents like jasmine and rose. They

Traditional artifacts find a modern sensibility when used out of context. Here, the rail of a south Indian cradle becomes a towel rail (above), a *jharokha* (window frame) from a dismantled *haveli* (mansion) frames a bathroom mirror (right), and a *goumukh* (literally "cow's mouth") tap (left) speaks of the Hindu belief that the cow is a vehicle of divine energy and her mouth the source of the sacred river Ganges in the Himalayas.

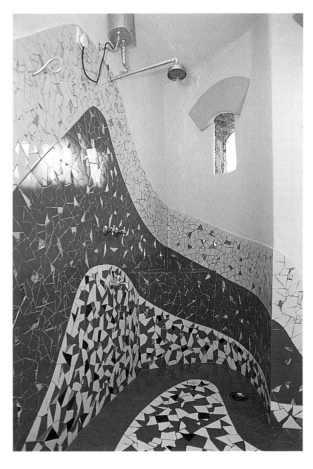

polish their skin with secret recipes conjured from mixtures of sandalwood paste, rosewater, or various fruits like mango, pineapple, and coconut. Hair is given a glint of mahogany by using a paste of henna, and shampoos are made at home by boiling together a variety of herbs and roots.

The functional side of a bathroom is often tempered by an aesthetic one. Decorative objects line walls and shelves, clusters of brass oil lamps and gently glowing incense sticks suffuse the air with Eastern fragrances, and one is tempted to linger on and relax. Plants are used to bring the outside in, an effect that is simple to create; a fountain of ferns looks stunning when juxtaposed with a collection of bronze statues or tall vases that have, over the years, acquired a patina of age.

A palette of blues from sapphire to aquamarine imparts a watery serenity to each of these bathrooms. Granite (top left), china mosaic (bottom left), and tiles and marble (near left) add a cool brilliance, while an octagonal shower (right) placed daringly in the middle of a lush garden with only an *aspara* (celestial maiden) for company, makes an unlikely but enchanting outdoor bathroom. In Royina Grewal's book *In Rajasthan,* she describes the bathroom of the Shringar Mahal, where the Maharanis bathed themselves. "Guests often discover its open-air bathroom with a mixture of shocked delight and coyness: a louvred grill provides a view of the village from the toilet, while the shower stands among green shrubs and trees, with the ever-changing Rajasthani sky above."

space outside

on the terraces

Terraces in India are used for casual entertaining (above) or as a vantage point from which to enjoy the wind and the view (right). A marble, lotus-shaped fountain (opposite) rests during the monsoon but promises a cool respite in the hot months to follow.

Outdoor rooms—patios, verandas, balconies, courtyards, and enclosed gardens—are a beautiful feature of tropical and temperate dwellings throughout India, and can be transformed into stylish extensions of the home with cool colonial restraint or by employing full-blown Indian flamboyance and an abundance of color. The uses to which outdoor spaces are put depends as much on the personality of the dweller as on the potential of the space.

Many popular Indian films have romanticized the balcony, for it is from here that the hero woos the beautiful heroine on the opposite veranda under a starlit sky.

An eminent artist has built his dream home in the wilderness of Bhimpura. Here, a colorful dragon made of china mosaic sprawls along the roof terrace and gazes out at surrounding hills that are alive with wolves and panthers. The house is built on several levels, each of which opens onto a private terrace that can be used for relaxing or for entertaining. A secret swimming pool built on a higher level looks down over an incredible forest of foliage and flowers.

verandas and balconies

Almost all but the poorest Indian homes, whether the older bungalows or the modern city apartments, have a veranda or balcony. In India, dawn is a time for quiet introspection, and people start a new day with tea or breakfast on a balcony or veranda. Some colonial properties and townhouses are surrounded by long, narrow balconies, which tempt hot and weary visitors to rest a while, drink tea, or have a chat. These balconies also act as ventilators that allow cool drafts into the home to replace the torrid heat of stationary air.

In the towns and in villages, where many homes open out into a garden or the road, friends sit on balconies, watching street performances, vendors, and the life of the town go past. The old homes of Goa and the colonial mansions in Bombay and Madras still have very imposing porches out of which stretch lengthy verandas. These are often scattered with natural, gold, or white cane furniture, evocative

A hacienda-style home in Goa basks in the tropical heat.

of a bygone Britishness. Cane coffee tables appear to be waiting for a silver tea service replete with luncheon or snacks. Colored glass lampshades throw out charming multi-colored patterns, and it is easy to imagine liveried waiters bringing out glasses of sherry at dusk.

column styles

Many verandas are supported by uniquely styled columns. Each period in Indian history is marked by a particular kind of column, and all over India monuments with grand columns stand testimony to the eventful happenings of the past. In the third century B.C., the emperor Ashoka installed pillars carved with Buddhist teachings in many places in India. Pillars in some of the ancient temples of south India have been fashioned with such a magical combination of metals that when tapped with a thin metal rod, they each produce a different musical note. Some old columns and pillars in Hindu temples, like the *deepastambha* (*deepa* meaning light, *stambha* meaning pillar in Sanskrit) have little niches for oil lamps used on special occasions. Traditional Indian columns are enhanced with special motifs: the *ghatapallava,* or pot, the lotus, and the *chakra,* or wheel, are still seen as capitals on columns today. Entire columns are chiseled with scenes from the Hindu epics, myths, and stories. The national symbol of India, seen on currency notes and government documents, is a replica of the three-faced lion capital of the pillar at Sarnath built by the emperor Ashoka.

outdoor ornaments

Outdoor rooms are also the perfect place for positioning fountains of ferns and other refreshing plants. Huge urns—which began their existence as kitchen containers—are now used as gleaming planters, and each region of India boasts of a different size, shape, and material for these containers. The *uruli*, for example, a shallow, open-necked vessel used for making sweet rice pudding in Kerala, makes an excellent small lotus pond. The etched terra-cotta urns of Gujarat make ideal bases for occasional tables on a veranda.

Metal bells of varying sizes and of different levels of sheen—from burnished gold, copper, and bronze to deliberately dull—are used in many gardens and patios and as ornaments; originally, they would have been used in temple ceremonies. Wooden or terra-cotta bells add further texture and contrast richly with the smooth patina of metal ones. Strong light during the long daytime hours is diffused by trelliswork screens, which also provide support for creepers.

An easy seat to take a rest upon out of the glare of the sun (above). A traditional *vrindavan,* displaying the holy basil plant, is the focus of this typical south Indian red cement–tiled courtyard (left).

Courtyards paved
in raw brick or
stone bring an
element of the out-
doors into the
home. A rustic
camel chair with a
woven cane seat
(left) shares the
texture of the
rough floor and
wall, while a
smooth, creamy vat
provides visual
relief. A comfort-
able chair (right)
stands among
various oil lamps,
and a bamboo fan,
handy for swatting
an annoying fly,
hangs on a wall
nearby.

courtyards

In all traditional Indian houses, the courtyard (*angan*, in Hindi) is of great significance. The great painted doors of a Rajasthani *haveli*, or mansion, open into an atrium around which the rest of the mansion is built. In the south of India, the courtyard is like a large, open room in front of the house with a low wall or fence running around it. The dark teakwood ancestral homes of the Nair community in Kerala, called *tharavads,* enclose a precisely built geometric courtyard known as a *nalukettu*. This atrium is encircled with columned verandas and brass-studded teak doors, which are carved with flowers, birds, and images inspired by ancient religious stories.

In a country where every aspect of Hindu life is devoted to a deity, it is hardly surprising that such courtyards are used for daily ritual worship. Most Hindu courtyards proudly display a *vrindavan*—a decorated, tall, rectangular pot that holds the *tulsi*, or holy basil plant. Hindus consider the plant to be especially loved by Vishnu, one of the main Hindu deities, and it is held sacred.

This spirit of sanctity that begins at the entrance continues throughout a Hindu home, and is the underlying principle behind the custom of people removing their shoes before entering the house. Cleanliness and the necessity of keeping cool by walking barefoot on the floor play a part, but Hindus also believe

Southern style: the view from the central courtyard of a Chettinad house in Madras (above). A wooden Kerala mansion (right and left) has been carefully reconstructed in Bombay. Rangoli tiles pave the courtyard (left) and a large mirror from Uttar Pradesh reflects the southern architecture.

that the home is a temple and cannot be sullied with unclean material from outside, so rows of footwear are lined up in a corner of the courtyard.

In north India, the courtyard is the venue for the celebration of a very special Hindu festival: *Karwa-Chauth*. Most major Hindu festivals come around the time of the full moon; *Karwa-Chauth* is a women's festival celebrated in Punjab, Uttar Pradesh, and Madhya Pradesh, when married women of all ages dress up in their silks and jewels, then fast and pray through the day for the prosperity and long life of their husbands and children. When the moon is at last sighted in the dark autumn sky, the women bring deep plates filled with water into the decorated courtyard and gaze at the reflection of the full moon in the water. Only after this can they break their fast, which is done ritually by the husband, who offers the first morsel of food to his wife.

In many Indian homes, the line between inside and outside is blurred, as seen in this highly stylized veranda near Delhi (left). Richly bracketed columns and narrow wooden balconies sourced from a dismantled mansion have been resurrected among new architecture and lighting. An open view through high arched frames (above) almost makes this startling pavilion a little bit closer to heaven.

porches

Porches in Indian townhouses are often painted or marbled pavilions. In rural Karnataka, the stairs leading up from a porch are flanked by stone seats. In Goa, such porches are called *balcaos,* and they have a distinct Portuguese air about them. Busy, patterned tiles and geometric proportions are softened by stained-glass windows that throw light on cool, whitewashed walls. These *balcaos* are extended living rooms that can see lots of social activity each morning and evening but may be deserted in the afternoons which, being so hot, are reserved for the daily siesta. The colonial hill station mansions of south India have beautiful columned verandas fanned by gentle breezes carrying the fragrance of nutmeg and cinnamon from nearby plantations.

In India, open gardens are much more popular than enclosed ones, and city-dwellers may create gardens on the roof terraces of their homes. Roof terraces are used as open-air bedrooms in the summer, or decorated with potted plants and statues to double up as entertainment areas. Many of them have china mosaic floors in plain colors or patterns.

John and Faith Singh's Anokhi farmhouse in Jaipur, Rajasthan (pictured right), has a semi-enclosed courtyard that is lush with mango trees heavy with fruit, a cool lily pond, and a patchwork of brown-and-white tiles laid against cobalt blue ones. The patio that overlooks this courtyard is held up by a collection of columns, while cane furniture and marble-topped columns stand on a smooth terra-cotta–colored floor.

A young coconut plant welcomes visitors into this tiled porch (left), where a cool bench offers a place to rest. The door is constructed with independent panels that help control the amount of light and also affords privacy.

This farmhouse in Jaipur (right) is a kaleidoscope of color and texture, where ink blue meets brown and white, and silky marble challenges craggy stone. A stone seat here has views of both the courtyard and the garden.

space for transition

safe passages

Not all homes in India have a hallway, as it is quite common for the front door to open directly into the living room. Where corridors exist, they are usually little more than somewhere in an apartment where people take off their shoes before walking into the home to preserve its cleanliness and sanctity.

No home in India is complete without some representation of divinity. In a traditional Hindu home, a statue, icon, or painting of one or more deities is installed in the corridor, so that it is the first image you see as you enter the house and the last one you see as you leave. The most distinctive quality of the Hindu concept of godhead is that it is manifestly polytheistic, and people have collections of symbols that represent gods and goddesses in their homes. They worship, or consider sacred, many objects ranging from stones, trees, and fruits to stars, departed ancestors, and the male and female reproductive organs. A Hindu will often have a statue of a junior god called a *dwar-pal,* or gatekeeper, at the entrance to guard his home from evil. A Christian home has a small cross and a rosary that is flanked by votive candles.

motifs

Corridors in India often display mirrors that are framed with exquisite motifs like the grapevine, and beveled or etched with fruits and curlicues. People believe that when good luck comes to the door, its reflection in a mirror draws it into the home. Auspicious symbols like the full

A flight of steps is flanked by six wooden elephants, which have long symbolized strength, intelligence, and steadfastness (right). The main staircase to the apartment carries light with it as it ascends (above). An old wrought-iron spiral of stairs (opposite) leading to a roof terrace throws off dramatic mid-afternoon shadows.

pot of water called the *kumbha,* the mango, considered a symbol of desire and plenty, and the elephant echo throughout the hall. The elephant is respected for its great intelligence, grace, and gentleness, and can be seen painted or carved in different forms all over the country.

customs

The home's threshold is also quite often the venue for many Hindu customs. When entering her new home for the first time, a bride is asked to overturn a measure of rice with her right toe, spilling the grains from the door into the house to signify that she brings with her a surfeit of good luck and plenty. She is then asked to dip her palms in a mixture of *kumkum* (red powder used by Hindu women to paint a dot on the forehead) and water and mark the walls with an imprint of her hands. This again is considered to be a sign of good luck, and the bride is likened to the goddess Lakshmi, who is the harbinger of wealth and prosperity.

staircases

In Indian architecture, sweeping staircases have, for centuries, signified aspirations towards a higher spirit and finally towards self-realization and salvation. Temples always have a flight of steps leading to the inner sanctum, which holds the divine image.

Some early twentieth-century buildings have a spiral staircase on one side, used as a fire escape or perhaps a servants' entrance.

From the great, sculpted stone steps of ancient temples to the concrete stairways of a contemporary apartment, there is a breathtaking stylistic variety of staircase treatments. Old buildings all over the country still have wide, curving stairways made of teak or marble, but newer designs use materials like granite and even transparent acrylic to give a sense of space.

Balustrades and balusters also give rich scope for embellishment. Usually made of wood, they are carved or polished until smooth and satiny. Flowers, vines, and leaves in wood or metal often ascend the stairs through graceful balusters, and the wall by the staircase often becomes a private gallery where framed family photographs, collections of artifacts, and favorite groups of paintings are displayed.

A heavy, studded door reveals a shady pavilion on a roof terrace and is the perfect intermediary between the cool interior and the burst of sunshine outside (far left). Pierced windows or *jalis* allow cool breezes to enter a long, dark corridor (left top). Thick, creamy walls are the perfect foil for a jet-black granite stairway (right).

architectural
features

windows

The *Vastu Shastra* advises caution in the building and maintenance of windows. Broken panes or cracked window frames invite bad luck into the home.

jalis

Following Rajput tradition, many Indian windows were designed so that the women of the household would be afforded outside views but nobody could view them from outside. The Mughal rulers of India, who introduced the *purdah* system, built breathtakingly beautiful windows in their palaces for this very purpose. The segregated women's area, known as the *zenana,* was kept veiled and mostly indoors, but the women observed the outside world through their windows. The panels of these windows, which let in light and air, were called *jalis* and were often an intricately carved filigree of stone or wood, sometimes of metal or plaster.

The art of the *jali* carving was at times so fine that it resembled intricate lace. The Hawa Mahal, or Palace of the Winds, in Jaipur in Rajasthan state, has a complete façade of such pierced windows from which its women could view the bustling street below. *Jali* carvers take their inspiration from geometric designs and traceried trees and flowers.

The clean lines of a Gothic lantern of blue leaded glass are in stark contrast to the rustic stone wall in which it is set (above).

Bamboo *chicks* keeps the glare of the midday sun at bay while offering a hazy view of the columned veranda outside (right).

jharokhas

Some of the most beautiful windows in the whole of India are seen in Rajasthan and Gujarat. Crafted entirely out of wood, the entire window, including the surround, is known as a *jharokha,* and the frames, sills, and panes are all intricately carved. Sometimes people look for a *jharokha* in antique markets and mount it on a wall as a feature in its own right. The surround of a *jharokha* also looks equally stunning as a frame for a painting and can add a special old-world charm to antique works of art.

Where *jharokhas* are used as windows that open to the world outside, it is very easy to imagine an unseen almond-eyed, dusky beauty peering through as she awaits her lover, a picture that is painted by many Indian authors of romantic fiction.

internal windows

There is also a very special kind of window in India that is often built within the house, connecting adjoining rooms. Normally these take the form of an opening in the wall which, when left open, adds dimension to a room. Privacy can be recalled by drawing a light curtain around it.

Most common, of course, is the small service window between a kitchen and dining area.

stained glass

Another classic window treatment is the use of stained glass. From the old, colonial homes where fanlights, ventilators, and windows have colored glass of unsurpassed beauty, to modern homes where custom-made stained glass in any design or color can be seen, this is a popular and affordable look.

louvers and slats

Windows in India often have wooden shutters with louvers or oblique slats. This form of shade is shared by many Mediterranean countries and was probably brought to India by the Portuguese. Although they are most often left as polished wood or painted white, they can also be accentuated with color to match or contrast with the room.

independent shutters

In the south, where the sun is at its most intense, practical minds of the past developed shutters made up of six or eight horizontal panels. Each panel can be opened and shut independently, and in this way, the amount of light can be controlled perfectly. People in the hottest areas like their homes to be cool and semi-dark, and these shutters play a significant role in achieving that.

India has traditionally favored floor seating, and in some old houses windows stretch all the way to the floor, resembling glass doors. In the days when life was less hectic, people would sit at ground level and gaze at verdant gardens and trees laden with juicy, tropical fruits. In the drawing room, these windows would overlook the path approaching the front door so that preparations for the welcome of visitors could start in advance. It is still possible to find these

This fretwork of *jali* (near right) incorporates geometric motifs seen in ancient and modern architecture all over India. Wooden louvers (far right) promote welcome ventilation.

Trompe l'oeil meets pattern and color in this Goan window, which provides the perfect place from which to observe a bustling street bazaar below (left). Yellow and blue is a common combination in the decoration of coastal homes in the south.

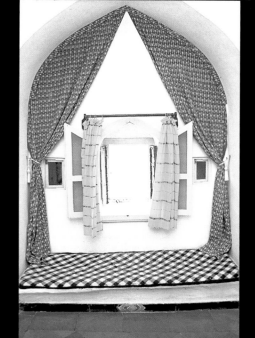

A series of pointed arches opens onto the arid Rajasthani landscape beyond (left). Striped yellow cotton curtains sway lazily and provide highlights against the stark black and white checked bedspread.

Even security bars can be decorative, as in this enthusiastic display of form and shape. Grilles are popularly used all over India for safety and ventilation. Here, strong bowlike shapes create a contemporary *jali* (right).

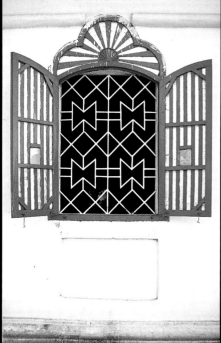

A Gothic grille of wrought-iron covers a bathroom window and cages an unsuspecting reindeer lost in a far-away tropical place (right).

A simple white wooden window opens to reveal miles and miles of breathtaking greenery sprinkled with gold dust by a mid-morning sun (left). Rural embroidery colors, patterns, and techniques join forces (right) in this window.

The lavishly arched and studded window (main picture) is typical of a rural style that is seen in states as diverse as Gujarat and Uttar Pradesh. Many decorative styles of India share a cross-cultural identity.

A fine *jali* window seems almost out of place set into this rough, weathered wall (above). It was formerly used to preserve the privacy of the women of the house.

Stained glass is extremely popular. Traditional stained glass techniques are often applied to contemporary designs (right).

windows, which usually have four shutters that can be opened separately to give an overview or a floor-level view. In the north, these windows have frames inspired by Islamic arches and are fitted with panes of colored glass in vivid hues of blue, red, or yellow, and sometimes tiny flower forms or geometric patterns are introduced in the glass.

windowsills

Making the most of the natural light, broad windowsills are sometimes converted into dressing tables by placing an ornate oval mirror, glass vials of perfume or cosmetics, silver-edged combs and brushes, and a few *objets d'art*. They also make a great place for arranging an altar or for creating a space for worship with an assortment of idols, a lamp, and a couple of incense sticks. Indians always decorate their altar with fresh flowers and these are delivered to the home each day. Rose petals, marigolds, and lilies add color and fragrance and invoke a sense of divinity and peace.

If a windowsill is deep and wide, it may be used as a window seat. A few cushions with cool white or bright, mirror-worked or sequined covers create a tempting corner ideal for solitary activity or repose.

chicks

Owing to the bright Indian light outdoors, shades and curtains take on special significance. Beautiful *chicks* (screens made of bamboo and twine) and cane or bamboo roller blinds are extremely popular and add warm, neutral tones to a room. *Chicks* can also be painted with designs or given a wash of color to blend in with a room. They contribute a certain

translucent effect to the window, which has the advantage that outdoor views are not completely barred from within.

grilles

Grilles are another feature of windows in many Indian homes. In some parts of Bombay, there are superlative examples of Art Deco style. Grilles in geometric lines, sun-ray designs, cubes, waves, and triangles are a legacy of colonial times that offset the more traditional icons of gods and goddesses. During the 1930s and '40s, Bombay enjoyed a boom in the building industry. This was also the time when wealthy Indian entrepreneurs were enjoying the fruits of colonization and were really living it up in the best tradition of a Western lifestyle. Cabaret, fashion, music, and food all lent a Western sensibility to traditional Indian living and the moment was ripe for the introduction of Art Deco style, which was all the rage abroad. The new style took root and expanded rapidly, fast replacing the fashion for Victorian influences. Today many buildings with Art Deco metalwork on windows and balconies are preserved for posterity.

diwali decoration

For the Hindu festival of *Diwali* in early November, Hindus decorate their homes by hanging a waterfall of fairy lights onto grilles, hanging flower garlands, and placing tiny oil or wax lamps, called *diyas*, in a row on the sill or floating them in a decorative bowl of water. At the window of each house, in view of passersby, often hangs an illuminated paper lantern, the most favored shape being the star. This sight is most commonly seen in Bombay.

thresholds

A festive front door (above) with garlands of marigolds and fresh mango leaves and two southern *apsaras*, or celestial maidens, awaits the arrival of an honored guest. A pierced door echoes and multiplies a floor pattern (right). An old door from a mansion in Gujarat (far right).

The *Vastu Shastra* gives advice on door design. It compares a house to the human body and the front door to the mouth. As we think of eating good food that is filling as well as nutritious, so also good and noble thoughts should enter the home. In the same way that the body processes food and rids itself of waste from the rear, the house should have smaller doors within and the back door should be in line with the front door to dispose of any residual, evil energy. This system of placing doors will lead to the prosperity and peace of all the inhabitants.

The abstract concept of opening a door to embrace the good that lies on the other side is at the heart of Indian philosophy and it is repeated in the scriptures of every religion. In Hinduism, ceremonial worship begins with the opening of the temple doors to reveal the silk-robed, bejeweled god within, an act that is symbolic of the opening of heaven. These temple doors are embellished with images of lesser, intermediary gods. And in all places of worship the ritual opening and closing of doors at certain times has special significance. Temple doors are often low or heavy to symbolize the hardships one must overcome to attain salvation.

rural entrances

The front door of a home is equally important. In a country where sometimes the next house is miles away, a door may only be needed as a barrier against sun and rain and the odd wild beast. In the sandy landscapes of Rajasthan and Gujarat, a door can merely be a length of brightly colored fabric, shot through with silver or gold and encrusted with thousands of tiny mirrors. Through the length and breadth of India, doors range from the essence of simplicity and elegance to ones that are richly carved examples of wood or metal.

chettinad doors

In the south, which is truer to the Hindu tradition than the north, thick wooden doors are framed with details of gods and goddesses worked in relief. Chettinad, near the temple town of Madurai in Tamil Nadu, produces some

of the most intricate doors in the south. Chettinad doors and frames have elaborately carved panels that rise above the frame, sometimes up to two feet high, which are embellished with symbols of good luck and prosperity. These were favored by the Chettiyar trading community of the region from the mid-nineteenth to the early twentieth century, when they enjoyed a particularly prosperous spell. Some Chettinad doors are like many other rustic ones: low in height. The idea was that people had to bow to enter through it and were therefore reminded to give respect to their hosts.

madras welcome

A collector of brass lamps from Madurai in the southern state of Tamil Nadu lives in a Chettinad-style house in Madras. As one approaches her front porch, a beautiful Chettinad door becomes visible through a forest of pillars. The door itself is the color of dark mahogany and is carved with the ten incarnations of Lord Vishnu, the god of creation in Hindu mythology. The top panel extends outwards in front like a little roof and every evening tiny oil lamps are lit near the threshold to symbolize the entry of good thoughts and goodwill into the home.

rajasthani havelis

The *havelis,* or mansions, of Rajasthan have beautifully painted double doors with tiny but perfect interpretations of traditional stories. Popular themes include Krishna and Radha disporting near lotus-dotted ponds, or a classical heroine looking longingly at rain-filled clouds bearing the promise of romance. Many of these

paintings, known as *pichwais*, are done in brilliant colors on a black or dark backdrop, and such doors look quite stunning against the natural, mud-stained walls.

gujarati wooden doors

Gujarati homes, too, are adorned with carved wooden doors. A famous architect who has made a home in Ahmedabad receives his guests at a typical Gujarati door. Studded with wooden flowers that surround a rectangular mirrored panel at the center, the door is dark and heavy, and makes a dramatic statement at the entrance to this beautiful home. Leaves, flowers, and parrots are favorite decorative motifs in Gujarati work; these legendary messengers of love in Indian folklore are chiseled to curl around the edges of a solid wooden door.

auspicious motifs

Ganesha, the elephant-headed god of wisdom, holds pride of place at the entrance to a Hindu home, and there are literally hundreds of interesting forms of this much loved deity, who is particularly popular in the Bombay area. Other motifs in western India include luscious cobs of corn, heavy bunches of grapes, and plump mangoes intertwined with creepers and tendrils to frame paneled doors and to suggest exotic plenty.

maharashtrian mansions

In Maharashtra, the old *wadas,* or mansions, have tall doors flanked by slim circular columns usually topped with an inverted lotus capital. These doors are typically paneled, and each panel is studded with a shining brass button. These studs are fashioned in the shape of

A *toran*, or bunting, of gold foil mango leaves, tiny oil lamps, and a simple *rangoli* announce an auspicious event (above). Colonial influence is at its best in this glass and metal door in Bombay (opposite) where curling grillework creates a tough silhouette in the afternoon sunlight.

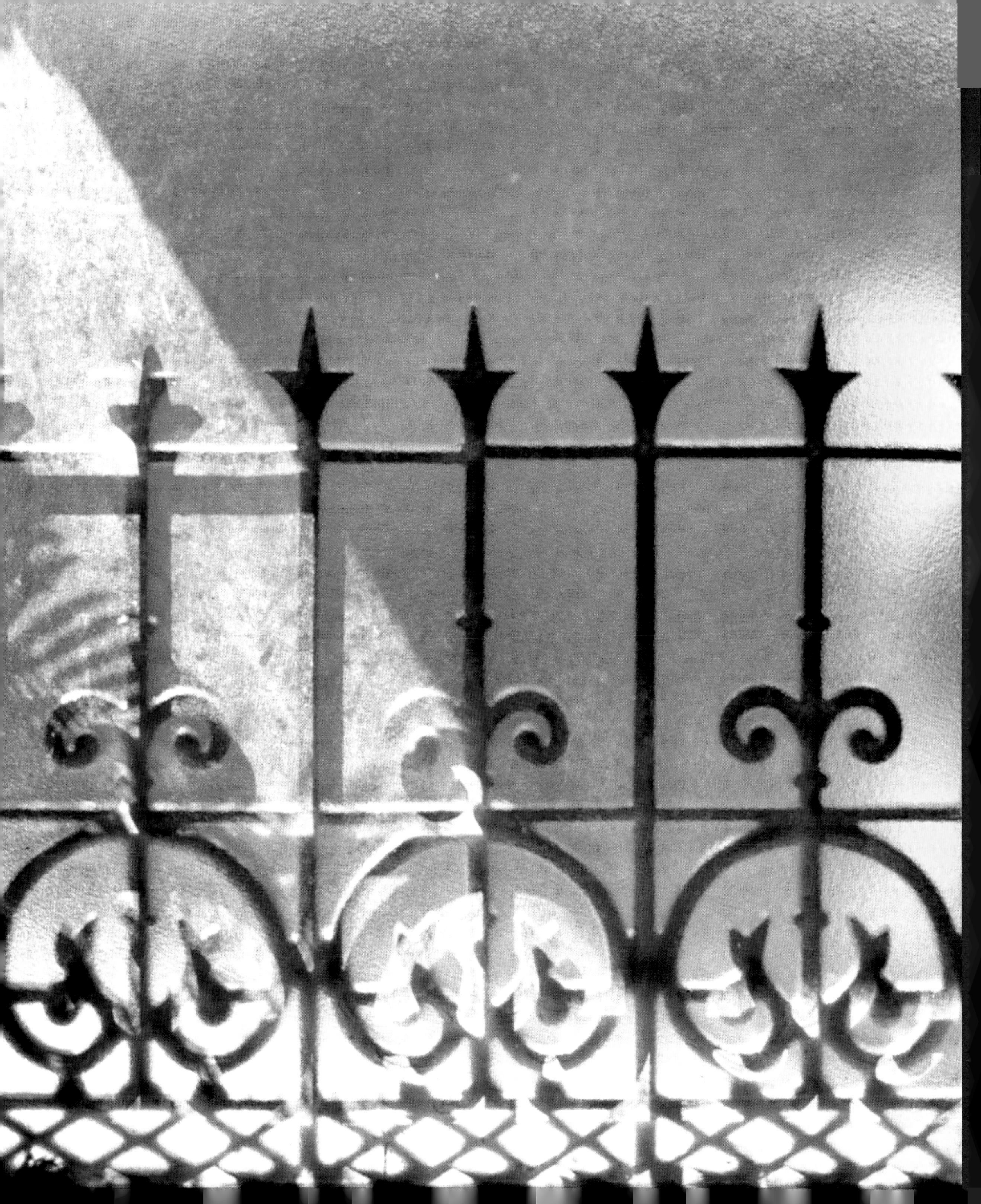

Vanilla doors with beaded icing make a sumptuous entrance to this large colonial style bathroom, which could be anywhere in the world but for the group of artifacts crowding an arched niche (above).

flowers, squares, stars, or geometric shapes, and are often left unpolished. The door is crowned with a wavy arch that contains the family crest or other auspicious symbols such as the lotus or the coconut. Long, slim spirals of smooth, wrung wood, almost like dark chocolate icing, surround the actual door.

kerala style

In Kerala, wood is used extensively in the home, and the doors are quite unique for the locking system they use. Traveling down the Malabar coast, there are breathtaking examples of large doors secured with ornamental *maniputte* locks, which have a clever intrinsic lever framework, so that if a wrong key is inserted a warning bell rings, almost like a medieval alarm system. *Maniputte* locks are very large and often in the shape of an arrow or anchor. A Hindi film producer living in Bombay has re-created a house based on the design of his family home in Cochin. The large doors, guarded by stern-looking security men, are bolted with an oversized, shiny *maniputte* lock. Interestingly, many Kerala doors have no metal hinges; they work on a wooden pivot mechanism held together without nails.

mughal influence

North India has absorbed the strong Islamic influences of its erstwhile Mughal rulers, and these are seen in everything from literature to architecture. Cusped arches, fluted minarets, and onion-shaped domes crown doors that maintain privacy and ensure the segregation of men and women. The typical Muslim arch seen in India shares a common style with arches in the Middle East and Turkey.

colonial homes

In the old colonial homes of Goa on the west coast, former French settlement Pondicherry in the southeast, and the British hill station of Simla in the north, glass doors afford outside views but maintain the tranquillity within. Typical features include quaint, fretted spandrels, leaded glass panes, and etched or engraved panels of clear, stained, or frosted glass. Some of these old houses reveal magnificent examples of vibrantly colored stained glass—geometric patterns and florals being the favored designs. Today, interest in stained glass is enjoying a much-deserved revival, and contemporary homes are also embellished with it. Expanses of stained glass look like exquisite frescoes; a tropical sun also ensures that the interior of the home is washed with jeweled colors.

All over the country, front doors provide an opportunity for embellishment. They serve to divide spaces, to add to the character of the building, and to exhibit the tastes and prefer-ences of the owner. Some people lean towards metal- and brass-studded doors, which are considered to be symbols of wealth. Certain auspicious symbols in wood relief or metal are said to invite good fortune into the home. Lions, bulls, and horses evoke power and wealth, whereas flowers and birds are reminiscent of things gentle and graceful.

Orange, brown, and yellow create an elaborate environment for this faux shuttered door (left). The frame has been painted by Ritu Nanda (who owns Camelot, a prestigious homeware shop in Goa), with the help of artist Luigi Anastesia.

In the days of the maharajahs, this scalloped doorway would have been shaded not by a bamboo *chick* as seen here (left), but by a hazy screen of woven *vetiver*, a fragrant grass, that not only cooled the interior but scented it too.

Simple rural artistry in its full uninhibited glory (right). Urban tastes may find this door excessive, but the electric blue has a purpose: it symbolizes the Hindu god Krishna and the romantic monsoon, when wild peacocks dance with joy.

A strong wooden door is painted coral to reflect the blazing sun and earthiness of this home (right). It derives its design from the heavy gates of old forts, where studs and metal strips were used for added strength.

Shiny chocolate brown is in contrast to a cream and lemon surround in this south Indian doorway (left). According to the *Vastu Shastra*, the main door should be bigger than all the other doors to invite good luck inside.

This highly ornamental door (left), with its abandon of motif and color, is completely comfortable in its rustic surroundings. It shares a commonality of adornment with temple doors of Gujarat and Rajasthan.

taj mahal style

The greatest work of Islamic architecture in India is the Taj Mahal, which has inspired many lesser doors. The Taj has creamy marble walls inlaid with a graceful Persian pattern of precious jewels, which has influenced a certain style of enamel work that is sometimes seen on other beautiful and expensive doors. A structured mosaic of tiny colored shapes on metal is called *meenakari,* and this is done with honey-colored topazes, purple amethysts, emeralds, and turquoises.

customs

The main door also acts as a threshold within which certain rituals and customs become extremely important. The most important Hindu ritual associated with a new home is the cere-monial entry for the first time. This is known as *Griha Pravesh* and has to be done at a predetermined, auspicious time. People consult astrologers and *Vastu* experts to set the date and time, which is called a *muhurt* or *mahurat.* Only entry at such a sacred time will ensure the lasting happiness of the inhabitants. The *Griha Pravesh* should be during the day and in particularly favorable months. The owner of the home carries a *kalash* or metal pot, filled with water and crowned with mango leaves and a coconut, to signify immortality as they enter their new home. The *kalash* stands for the legendary *amrit,* or nectar of immortality, which, according to Hindu myth, the gods consumed in order to live forever.

A traditional Hindu housewife will ceremonially welcome an honored guest or relative, a newly married couple, or a new mother at her door with *arti*. A decorative plate with an oil lamp, some *kumkum* (red powder), a little rice, and a piece of *mithai,* or Indian sweet, is waved in little circular movements in front of the guest's face. She then applies a dot of red *kumkum* on the forehead, sprinkles a few grains of rice over the head, and offers the sweet. In the north, this custom is called *tikka lagana,* and sometimes *paan*—a betel leaf stuffed with spices, fruits, and herbs—is also offered.

festivals

On festive days, the doors and their surrounds may be decorated. Just outside the door, the housewife draws a pattern of auspicious motifs, geometric configurations, or floral designs on the floor. In south India, this is done with a paste of rice flour and water called *kolam.* In the west and north, a fine, white chalklike powder is used to draw the outline, and is filled in with various colors. This is known as *rangoli* (see page 142), and women have friendly competitions to judge whose work is the best. During *Diwali*, the festival of lights, every other door is decorated with *rangoli* designs featuring lamps, lanterns, mangoes, and coconuts. The Parsee community also embellish their doorsteps with *rangoli*. A scaly fish, which is considered to be a bearer of good luck, is one of their favorite *rangoli* motifs. For Parsee New Year, celebrated in March, butterflies and stars are drawn outside the home.

torans

All the communities of India decorate their doors with garlands on ceremonial days. Strings of mango leaves and saffron-colored, fragrant marigolds are hung in gentle loops on the door. These are called *torans*. However, *toran* is also the term applied to the various cloth, metal, or paper buntings that are hung over the door. Scallops, triangles, and inverted arches are most often used in *torans,* and each state has its *toran* specialty. Floral *torans* are made to order in a particular color or with an array of vividly colored flowers.

Doors weathered by the elements (left). A *maniputte* lock from Kerala (below) secures a door with its unique alarm system. A shiny sun-and-moon motif brass knocker adorns a polished Chettinad door (top right).

inviting the gods in

Gods and goddesses, especially those that govern wisdom, learning, and wealth, are constantly tempted or invited into the home. Many people draw a tiny set of footprints facing the door to symbolize the entry of the goddess Lakshmi, the bringer of material wealth, who is portrayed as standing in a pink lotus showering gold coins on her devotees. Sometimes the front door is left ajar to signify a welcome for this much propitiated deity. Similarly, one sees red handprints on and around many doors in the villages of India. These are made with *kumkum* and serve to declare good news or the happening of an auspicious event, usually a marriage or a birth, to people passing by.

room division

Doors between rooms are much more informal than the front door of the house. Often this division is accomplished simply by means of a sheer, light curtain, which allows cool air to circulate through the house. Privacy is not prized, and in many homes, only young married couples shut the bedroom door at night.

decorative details

walls

The lore of *Vastu Shastra* suggests that images of gods and goddesses should be decorated with garlands and hung in any room into which visitors are welcomed. This is to ensure that positive energies are attracted into the home, rather than ill will.

color

Throughout India, combinations of color are used spectacularly: aquamarine, ochre, saffron, indigo, pistachio green, shocking pink, pomegranate red, and mango yellow. The use of primary colors is often symbolic. Red is the color of Kama, the god of love and passion, and invites romance. Yellow is a reflection of the abundant sunshine, and is a color that is typical of homes in the town of Pondicherry in south India. Also, according to *Vastu,* yellow walls signify a mind that is inclined towards divine perception and intelligence. Blue is the color of the heavy monsoon and, of course, Krishna.

Red (above and right) is also the color of Agni, the god of fire, passion, and energy.

In Goa, homes are typically white or indigo. In Rajasthan, natural indigo is used to color walls a bright blue, while in Jaipur, walls are distinctively pink. Mud washes applied to homes in the rural villages stain walls a natural burnt sienna or dull red.

pierced walls

Many Indian homes in the villages and towns have pierced walls to let in light and air. The *jali*, or latticework, of the fabled Taj Mahal inspires contemporary screens that are usually made of marble or wood. Kashmiri wooden screens, embellished with images of the maplelike chinar leaves, are quite exquisite and make wonderful room dividers.

Cane screens divide the space by enclosing a room (far left) or by promoting privacy (left) and adding to the dull gold decor of the room. A *deepalaxmi* (goddess of light) is framed by a bare tree and a saffron wall (below).

Niches are used to display images of favorite deities. In modern homes, they also display more profane likenesses such as this mustachioed Rajasthani man (*right*).

Sheer fabrics and pierced screens serve the same purpose of deliberately tantalizing the eye and tempting the gaze to linger. In Mughal times, the harem would sit behind such resplendent lacy screens to watch court performances.

niches

Alcoves cry out for special lighting and are made into spectacles along with their contents. They are often used as shrines where tiny statues of favorite deities, religious symbols, or lamps and candles are placed, and offered fresh flowers each day.

stone walls

In places where it is very hot, especially in the central plains of north India, thick stone walls help to insulate the home from the summer heat. Marble is often chosen for its smooth, cool feel and neutral color, and huge slabs are sometimes inlaid with other marbles to create patterns. Granite also gives relief from the heat; the rock is usually polished to a mirror finish for a sleek look. Indian marble quarries produce an enormous range of hues, from the white and pink of Makrana to a black from Bhaisalana and ubiquitous and luxurious green and Udaipur pink.

stonework

Sandstone has a rough, grainy look and can be easily worked to incorporate carvings and sculptures. Many Rajasthani *havelis,* or merchants' mansions, have sandstone walls in red, ochre, and beige. Edwin Lutyens, the English architect who planned the Presidential Residence in New Delhi, used Dolpur red and beige sandstone. In Goa, walls of laterite— a baked clay, naturally colored yellow or red with iron pigments—give buildings earthy colors.

Of course, the skill of local carvers and stonemasons is well recorded in the many examples of breathtakingly beautiful carved walls in north India. Jaiselmer in Rajasthan is one of the jewels of carved stonework in the whole of the world, where pierced walls are quite astounding.

wooden construction

In the cool hill stations, walls are covered with wood paneling, which creates a feeling of

warmth. In the state of Uttar Pradesh, rooms are sometimes divided by carved and polished screens. Some of the old homes in Kerala, built almost 200 years ago, have walls made of wooden slats constructed so as to allow the welcome passage of cool breezes. Throughout India, craftsmen use many types of wood, depending on local availability, although indigenous teak is the favorite.

A bold blue wall matches the color of a Rajasthani chair and leads the eye through the doorway to the space beyond (above).

mirrorwork

All Indians love shine and glitter, and mirrorwork is therefore truly prized. Mirrored walls conjure visions of Kutch and Gujarat: the Banni tribe are well known for their round houses, and create mirrored masterpieces on their white lime and clay walls.

wall painting

In the villages of Rajasthan, on the road from Delhi to Jaipur, the array of painted homes gives the villages the appearance of elaborate art galleries: peacocks dance on walls, gods and goddesses frolic, and flowers bloom in the bountiful vigor of spring. Shekhavati is especially celebrated for its *havelis* painted with powerful elephants, graceful horses, and palanquins carrying beautiful damsels.

The Warli tribe of Maharashtra decorate their huts with stark white images on matte terracotta walls. Representations of trees, birds, and people going about their daily tasks crowd the canvas in a simple geometric style. Warli paintings

are now available as small wall hangings, plaques, and even on trays and table linen, and tribal art has caught the fancy of people decorating their homes in India's middle class, urban sector.

In the south, wall paintings are drawn on plaster, a technique evident in the region's many temples. The various tribes of the northeast paint pictures on their walls for different reasons. The Monpas follow Buddhism and draw Buddhist images on wooden panels. The Santhals use wall paintings purely as decoration; the Saoras draw a pantheon of gods, celestial beings, and ghosts to flatter them and keep them happy. Madhubani in Bihar is famous for its frescoes of people, animals, birds, and trees in compelling pinks and yellows. In Orissa, Lord Jagannath—a local form of the god Krishna—takes pride of place in wall paintings.

Traditional wall paintings in contemporary settings. A tribal Warli painting (left) from Maharashtra, and mythical Madhubani creatures (below) from Bihar. A Mughal "tree of life" on pistachio (opposite) enlivens the walls of a Shekavati *haveli* in Rajasthan.

floors

In India, the relationship of man and the earth is intense and the ground is revered: an Indian dancer salutes the earth and asks for blessings before stamping on it during rehearsal or performance. The earth is seen as a Mother Goddess, imbued with the power of procreation, from which comes food, the sustenance of all life.

raw elements

Wall-to-wall carpeting is eschewed by bare feet in favor of the cooling surface of a smooth floor; these are finished in a number of ways. In most of rural India, a mixture of mud and cow dung, said to be cleansing, is spread evenly and left to dry. This procedure is repeated every few weeks to maintain the floor, and the floor only needs occasional sprinkling with water to keep it neat and to damp down the dust.

More sophisticated dwellings use raw stone in which all the natural qualities of color, roughness, and shape are preserved.

marble

Marbled flooring is very popular. Inspired by the innumerable palaces, small and large, marble slabs are available in *lakhs* (tens of thousands) of colors and sizes. Marble looks opulent, as the rock has a radiance that is apparent even before polishing. Today, marble in all kinds of colors comes from Rajasthan and expensive varieties are also imported from Italy to furnish exclusive homes. Marble is in such demand all over the country that a huge distribution business operates in most major cities.

Like marble, terrazzo is available as large tiles or slabs. It is made of marble chips and dust, set in cement and colored. Terrazzo comes in various shades, from bold to metallic, and is still used widely.

cooling stone

Pleasing patterns are achieved by juxtaposing marble slabs with chips of contrasting hues and shapes. Many homes in India have floors of Jaisalmer stone, which is rich gold in color and

comes from Rajasthan. Stone floors are prized, as they keep the room cool; various kinds of stone from gray Kotah and Cuddapah to limestone to pink Jaipur stone are used to add a rugged aesthetic to cool, airy homes.

In south India, cement is used in its smoothest form, colored green or terra-cotta to match the natural colors in the landscape. This floor is pulled into the skirting as well, and is kept gleaming by wiping it down daily by hand.

Granite is also used to add richness and color. Most Indian granite, which is available in tan or black tones, comes from Rajasthan and the south.

hardwood floors

Although it is a dwindling resource, high quality hardwood is still found in abundance in India. Native teak, rosewood, sandalwood, shesham, and deodar are all used in the home. Wooden floors are warm and resilient, but can be rather noisy and need repeated sealing and polishing.

Herringbone parquetry contributes a formal, systematic geometry to hill station homes. In north India, softwood pine floors reflect soft golden light into the room. Kashmir, where houseboats provide many people with permanent accommodation, has delightfully perfumed cedarwood floors that help to warm the environment.

floor tiles

Today, checks, fleur-de-lys, honeycomb, and flowered tile floors, laid down sixty years ago, remain in many homes. Tiles are a unique feature of Goan homes, and some older bungalows have ancient Portuguese or Italian tiles that still look as glowingly fresh as when they were first installed.

Indian floor tiles are usually a muted yellow in color. Burnished to a silky smoothness by the constant passage of feet, these tiles are reminiscent of an age of subtle elegance when they were more widely used.

china mosaic

Some old homes have quaint mosaic floors, also known as glass mosaic, in which bits of crushed crockery and china are embedded in plaster to make colorful patterns that reflect light and create a dazzle underfoot. Associated with Byzantine architecture, this style spread from Asia Minor to Eastern Europe, Syria, Iraq, and

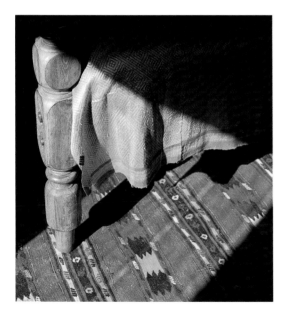

Until the 1930s, many *galicha* tiles (opposite) were imported from Italy; today they remain a historic feature. Instant interest is created by a cotton ikat *dhurrie* (near left), or a tribal-print carpet laid on satiny Jaiselmer stone flags (above).

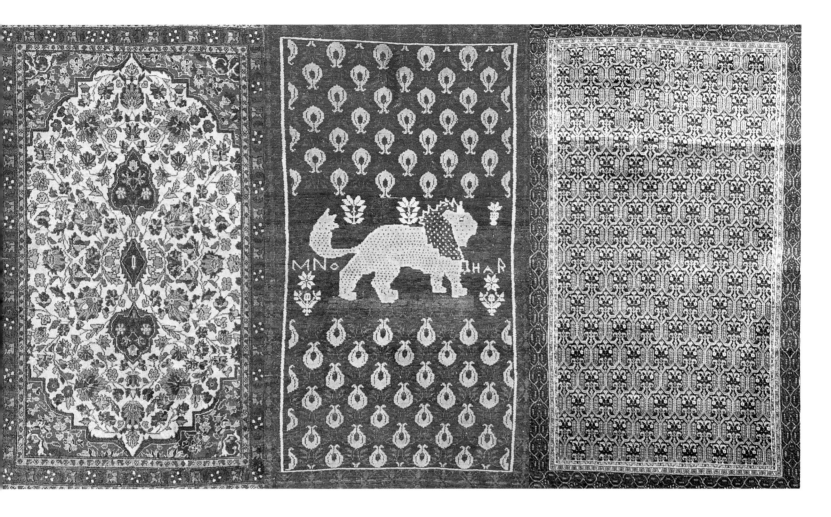

some parts of Persia (Iran). In India, it was promoted by the Mughal Emperor, Shah Jahan. In the cities, china mosaic is most often seen on verandas or open terraces.

rangoli and kolam

Anyone who has been to India will have seen the beautifully decorated painted patterns on the ground or the floor outside peoples' homes. *Rangoli* (Hindi) or *kolam* (Tamil) is the art of drawing birds, flowers, tendrils, or geometric configurations onto the floor with a paste of rice flour and water, with chalk, or with

watercolors. An outline is first drawn in pure white and then filled with colors, or left on its own to depict auspicious symbols or objects of beauty. A *rangoli* is conventionally painted on festive days, but some communities, including the Parsees and many people in south India, do this as a daily ritual. Sometimes a fine white powder called *rangoli* powder is applied, which requires great dexterity and suppleness of the fingers. A pinch of powder is gathered between the thumb and the index finger, and fine, sharp designs are traced out on plain, dark floors. In the cities, a small section of the floor is given a special mud wash that emulates a typical village floor, so that the white stands out in bold contrast.

Rangoli is associated with *Diwali,* when each home has a pattern outside the front door as a gesture of celebration and welcome. The women have friendly competitions to decide whose *rangoli* is the best.

carpets and rugs

Carpets are associated with luxury and grandeur and were introduced to India by the Persian Mughal emperors during the seventeenth century. Rugs were used as prayer mats by the Muslims but were also a valuable commodity, as well as a piece of portable furniture. Kashmir, with its verdant valleys, has always been ideal for rearing sheep, and produces the finest wool. From here the art spread all over the north, from Punjab to Uttar Pradesh and Rajasthan.

Carpets that are geometric in pattern are inspired by Islamic nomadic designs, whereas those that have exuberant curves and spirals steal shapes from flowers, fruits, trellises, and other natural elements from the gardens of the Mughal rulers—Islam, of course, does not allow the reproduction of human or animal forms. Most carpets are knotted in wool or silk, but cotton is often added to increase durability. Each carpet is evaluated by the number of knots per square inch. The greater the number, the more clarity the design will have. A good quality carpet should have between 150 and 300 knots per square inch. Take care when buying an antique carpet. Originally, only vegetable dyes like indigo and walnut were used, so an "antique" carpet with lilac, smoke gray, rose pink, or silver in its design is probably a fake!

dhurries

Indian *dhurries* are flat rugs more commonly made of cotton but also fashioned from silk and wool. They are woven with a warp and a weft, unlike carpets, which are knotted. Today they are produced in villages all over India. Modern *dhurries* use chemical as well as natural organic dyes, but they are no match for those produced in the eighteenth century, which have a simple elegance in their clear, frugal designs and color schemes. The Indian government banned the export of these antiques in the early 1990s, successfully increasing their appeal and their value.

grass matting

Perhaps the most common floor coverings of all are the *chatais,* or grass mats. In rural homes, this makes an unlikely but convenient mattress that is unrolled during siesta time on hot afternoons or at night, but rolled up and kept in one corner at all other times. A *chatai* is also considered essential when entertaining guests or inviting elders to sit down, as offering them a seat on the bare floor is almost an insult.

coir mats

If there is any kind of wall-to-wall floor covering in India that blends with the rest of the decor, is easy to maintain, and does not give off heat, it is coir matting, woven on traditional hand looms. This is most often found in natural pale golden shades, but can also be bought in a wide range of colors. Coir matting not only adds color but texture as well, and is woven in patterns such as concentric squares, circles, or herringbone. Kerala produces the finest coir mats.

The distinctive characteristic of a cotton *ikat dhurrie* is the geometric design, as in this example from Bombay, where a fiery gold and red pattern warms an ice-blue silk sofa (above).

textiles

Textiles are used all over the home in countless ways. They can be spread on the floor, draped over furniture, floated across windows, and cascaded down walls. A length of fabric and a little imagination can transform a room. The choice of Indian textiles is endless and the pleasure to be had from them immense. Experimentation with colors, patterns, textures, and motifs reveals the astonishing medley of seemingly incompatible and separate elements of color and form that create the rich tapestry of Indian fabric.

Since time immemorial, India has been known for its cloth, so rich and fine that several colonial conquerors were lured to her shores merely in the hope of getting hold of it. The cultivation of cotton and fashioning it into clothing originated in India. Records left by the Greek physician Ctesias, who lived during the fifth century B.C., showed that Persians of that time wore dyed and printed Indian cotton. Ancient Arabs and Egyptians knew cotton as *sindon*, the fabric that came from the land of the river Sindhu, later called the Indus. Gossamer-fine cottons dyed with iridescent vegetable dyes in various motifs were exported to countries all over the world.

motif and color

Texts dating back to the first century B.C. describe in detail cloths that are known by their colors: thus *nila* was indigo blue cloth, *lohitaka* was madder red, *kalaka* was black, and *laksa* was red from lac. This basic palette continued until pomegranate was combined with indigo to give dark green; iron shavings were stirred into vinegar to give black; and turmeric was rubbed onto fabric to produce a yellow stain.

With the influence of Islam from the twelfth century onwards, inspiration began to be sought from flowers and fruits, and subtler

Thick, embroidered silk (left) is used for upholstery or curtains to give a cool, elegant look. This fabric (right) is used for bridal wear in Uttar Pradesh, but can make a regal cushion cover. The profusion of pearls, sequins, and gold and silver thread embroidery speaks of Muslim artistry.

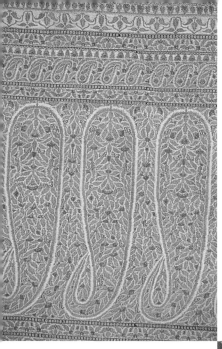

A Jamevar shawl of goat's wool strewn with elongated *kairis,* or paisleys, is typical of the fabrics of Kashmir (left), where each paisley is filled with flowers. The paisley motif developed from a design of a bouquet of flowers found in this beautiful region.

Rows of curling conches, elephants, and auspicious mythical birds known as *annapakshis,* which symbolize beauty, are woven in pure golden thread on this blazing red Kancheepuram silk (left). Doe-eyed goddesses in south Indian temples are dressed in similar saris.

A Gujarati silk patola (right) is considered lucky for the wearer. Gujarati weavers are known for their attention to detail, their fine pattern and color, and the intricacy of their work. Here, a clear sense of order arises out of a profusion of motifs.

Folk embroidery and mirrorwork from a Rajasthani village embellish this wall panel (right). Layer upon layer of design, in ever more circles, create a "garden" of flowers and leaves in the favorite colors of the region: pink, orange, and yellow.

South Indian silk brocade in contrasting colors of eggplant and tomato is embellished with a sweeping *kairl,* or mango, in gold thread (left). It is common to find an assortment of motifs within the same fabric.

A famous weave, *patola,* from Andhra Pradesh, is distinguished by the diffused forest scenes and birds and flowers (left). The fabric is shot silk, with red threads that are interspersed with green ones to produce a rust color.

Silver sequins and threadwork in Gujarati style bring out the beauty of a full lotus flower against a background of shimmering saffron velvet (left). Such fabrics are used for cushion covers, buntings, throws, or for decorating temples or altars in a home.

A fine tie-dyed silk called a *bandhani* is punctuated by ribbons of woven gold (left). A Gujarati bride wears such a cherry-colored sari, called a *gharchoda*, when she leaves for her husband's home after the wedding.

Hand-loomed fabric in a typical south Indian checked weave is divided by a wide band of swirls and creatures (right). This fabric in earth-rich colors comes from Andhra Pradesh, which is known for its weaving centers.

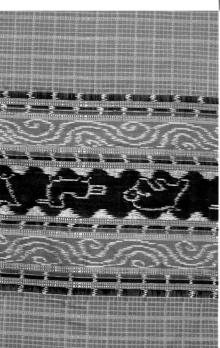

Meanders, flowers, and geometric shapes find their own corner in this Gujarati hand-embroidered cushion cover (right). Communities of rural women sew such covers in the village and travel to the cities to sell them.

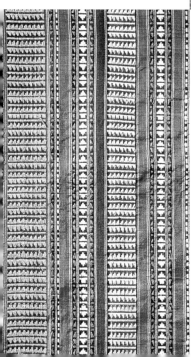

A traditional tribal fabric rich with color and weave (left). The tribes of northeast India use such striking shawls to protect themselves against the bitter Himalayan cold, as well as to decorate their frugal homes.

A fine example of *kantha* embroidery (left) from West Bengal brings to life an exotic "tree of life" with flowers, buds, creepers, and wild birds (left). Considerable time and skill is required for *kantha* work, and therefore it is very expensive.

shades like old rose, dove gray, and pale green from the pistachio began to be appreciated. The treatise of emperor Akbar (1560–1605), the *Ain-I-Akbari*, describes the colors of his wardrobe—divided according to the seasons—as ruby, golden, brass, grass green, cotton-flower, sandalwood, almond, grape, honey, parrot, apple, hay, mango, light blue, pink, violet, and musk.

dyeing techniques

Indian dyeing techniques are world-famous and have endured and developed through the centuries. A popular style of Gujarat is the *bandhani,* which is made by a traditional resist dyeing technique called tie-dye. *Bandhani* is produced in shocking colors; inspiration for combinations is drawn from nature, so red and yellow from the mango, or purple and green from the eggplant, are interspersed with irregular dots, squares, or triangles that result from the tie-dye process. Dyeing selectively waxed cloth—originally a Javanese technique—produces some of the finest batik in the world, which is used for clothes and soft furnishings. All the artisans involved in the dyeing and painting of cloth flourished until the end of the nineteenth century, when synthetic madder and

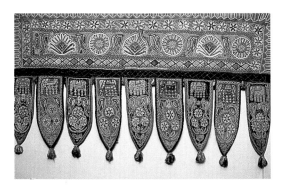

A colorful Gujarati collage enclosed by dotted *bandhani* in four corners incorporates detailed embroidery and mirror work (opposite). Gujarat also makes *torans* (left) to hang on the front door as a sign of welcome. A stepped doorway frames a cloth painting of the monkey god, Hanuman (above).

indigo, which were longer-lasting than their
natural counterparts, were discovered in
Europe, and machines that mass-produced
fabric were introduced into India. Before this,
beautiful handmade fabrics had been used
regularly to furnish palaces and royal tents, and
Indian kings and princes exchanged gifts of
exquisite cloth to honor each other.

weaving traditions

From early times, regional styles of weaving,
printing, embroidery, and painting on textiles
have also been well developed. Palaces and
tents of kings and queens were resplendent
with florals woven in gold and silver. In the
fifteenth century, weavers moved between Iran,
Turkey, and India, creating an artistic fraternity
that pooled and borrowed ideas and designs.
Today it is possible to distinguish the work of a
particular tribe, state, or community without
much effort. Although machine-made cloth is
now available in abundance, the true heart of
Indian fabric lies in the handwoven and

hand-worked textiles. Each state is famous for a
particular hand-loomed material, and very
specific handwork is easily identifiable.

patola—indian ikat

Possibly one of the most famous fabric weaves
of India is the *patola,* which is based on the *ikat*
technique of making parts of the yarn resist the
dye by wrapping. The wrapping is removed
before weaving the cloth on looms that are
made to face the weavers so that they can see
the woven patterns even as they work the
separately-dyed warp and weft together. *Patola*
is produced in Orissa, Andhra Pradesh, and
Gujarat.

embroidery and needlework

Hand-worked textiles are inevitably popular in a
country where labor is still relatively cheap.
Crewel and crochet work are done all over India
to produce lacy table linen and bedspreads.
Exquisite embroidery in triumphant colors is
the hallmark of village artisans, who produce

some of the most beautifully decorated cloth in the world. Gujarat is especially famous for its hand-worked fabrics. *Soof* embroidery, with its long, flat stitch, is much prized, as is the patchwork seen in quilts, cushion covers, and wall hangings. Embroidery here is not only done with thread, but cascades of sequins, twine, wire, and cowrie shells are also incorporated into the work.

western mirrorwork

The most famous feature of Gujarati and Rajasthani handiwork is the mirrorwork used on fabric. Round or square mirrors are stitched onto the cloth to make cushion covers, bed-spreads, wall hangings, and tablecloths. Mirrorworked material and artifacts are readily available in local shops and markets.

vibrant flowerwork

The best-known Punjabi handwork is the vibrant *phulkari* embroidery. *Phulkari* literally means "flowerwork" and it is done from the reverse of the fabric in satin stitches. The color scheme is almost always rich with shocking pink, saffron, red, yellow, and green silk floss thread, and the fabric is used for bedspreads and cushion covers. Geometric flowers, wheat sheaves, and leaves cluster together to consume a length of cloth. *Phulkari* work is ceremonially given to brides as a token of goodwill.

fragile patterns

The artisans of Lucknow in Uttar Pradesh make fragile, white embroidery patterns, called *chikan,* on pastel cottons. Many small-scale industries run by women make and sell tablecloths and napkins in *chikan* work.

the use of gold

Varanasi (Benares), in central India, produces the Benarasi sari as well as fabric with *zari,* or pure gold or silver embroidery, on silk. The Marwari community of Rajasthan is skilled in embellishing fabrics with a stiff gold lace called *gota.* This is stitched onto the border of a fabric to define it and add a touch of festivity.

block-printed fabric

Today the states of Gujarat and Rajasthan, and the town of Jaipur in particular, are the main centers of *chappai,* or printing. The technique of hand block printing on textiles is simple. A wooden block with one carved face is dipped in dye and pressed onto the cloth; this is repeated until the entire fabric is covered. Any variances in color are accepted as part of the art form.

upholstery. Rich, dark colors add drama and help to block the harsh tropical sunlight. Most Indians use jacquard for upholstery, and this comes mainly from Haryana, between Delhi and the Punjab, or from the south.

bed linen

Indian bed linen is available in a great variety of colors, textures, and materials. Pure cotton bedspreads in block-printed patterns come from Rajasthan. Lavish, single-stitch *kantha*-work covers from Bengal are produced by generations of women in a family tradition, and are very expensive. *Phulkari* bedspreads from Punjab are made in bright colors that draw the eye.

The most conventional way of dressing a bed in India is with a *kambal* or *razai*. In Gujarat, women sit for hours laboriously making patchwork *razais*—quilts—with squares of printed, embossed, or embroidered fabric in which gold and silver punctuate the color. In the rural region of Kutch, bedding is rolled up and stacked during the day and covered with a quilt or mirrorworked bedspread to make a prominent feature in the room.

cushions

Indian style delights in cushions. Thick bolsters covered in muslin or pure cotton are popular everywhere and adorn seating areas known as *baithaks*, swing chairs, and divans. Handmade mirrorwork from Gujarat; hand-painted Rajasthani cushions with miniature portraits of Krishna and Radha; embroidered flowers and creepers in powder pinks and blues from Kashmir; and the tiny diamond-shaped petals of white cotton (*patti-kam*) that adorn covers made in Lucknow—the list of designs is endless.

Vertical fabric blinds made of gentle cream and ecru appliqué work from Uttar Pradesh suggest a hint of pattern in the continuous wall (above). These curtains need never be opened, as they let in light and air and still afford a view of the terrace.

Centuries of colonialism and machine printing had all but killed this art, but Faith Singh, originally from Britain, dedicated her energies and her Rajasthani company, Anokhi, to its revival and brought contemporary designs and colors to the industry, thereby renewing international interest in block printing.

furnishing fabrics

Velvet, universally associated with wealth and glamour, comes from Surat in Gujarat and from Bombay. Its various forms, such as flocked velvet and velour, are used for curtains as well as for

curtains

Filtering and limiting natural light into the home is a necessity in India, and curtains of various materials are used. Softly gathered curtains in velvet, silk, or cotton are the most popular, although blinds made of thick *khadi* ("home-spun") cotton are also made into a feature in many homes. Unbleached cotton resembles a certain kind of *khadi*, and is sometimes used instead. Calico, which is fine cotton, provides hazy protection from the sun and is light enough to allow air to circulate around it. Saris made of calico or muslin are often fashioned into curtains. A tiny but prestigious hotel in Goa uses airy cotton saris with a thin blue border over the glassless windows of their "air" room.

paisley motif

The most significant motif that emerged from the textiles commissioned by the Mughals was the *buta,* a highly stylized version of a flower. The shape gradually evolved into the mango motif we know today as part of the paisley pattern, which takes its name from the town in Scotland where the trade was exported in the seventeenth century.

Silk hand-loomed saris from Orissa (yellow) and Tamil Nadu (blue and green) (above) make a fine curtain. They are sold all over India in state hand-loom shops and at annual fairs, and are also exported.

outside india

a hint of india

New uses for old: an old *patlo,* or low seat used for seating deities in a Hindu temple, which is converted into a newspaper rack (above); a faded but prized *toran* makes a colorful valance (opposite).

I hope that this book has inspired you to bring a touch of India into your home. The choice is enormous, but even a colorful *toran,* or a sari used as a throw, is a respectable beginning. There are no rules; authenticity need not be a criterion. It is also perfectly acceptable to mix southern, western, and northern design ideas: a terra-cotta pot from Tamil Nadu would never look out of place next to a Kashmiri screen, for instance. It is more important to get a feel for color, texture, and pattern.

Think of the five elements and introduce them into your decorative plan, making it a theater for light and air to play in. Experiment with the existing features of your home, and introduce new colors and motifs. Use rich saffron and majestic red boldly. Try serene and cooling ivory complemented with artifacts that have a hint of gold. Look for elephant- and lotus-shaped artifacts.

using color

Think of gold, silver, copper, and bronze and imagine the browns, reds, black, and rusts of Indian soil. The bright yellow of the mango, the dazzling green of the parrot, and the hot pink of bougainvillea all provide a rich palette to play with. The photographs in this book celebrate an uninhibited passion that Indians have for color and texture. Hopefully they will inspire you to try some of the ideas and color combinations yourself.

style heritage

Many of India's most effective interiors bring the country's design heritage into every corner of the home: traditional fabrics, woven to centuries-old patterns; pots crafted to a traditional template by the hand of a master potter; artifacts almost identical to those made by generations of craftsmen; and architectural details that resemble the ancient monuments of past emperors are represented all over India. Many authentic artifacts are also available outside India.

serendipity

Wander through antiques shops, markets, furniture stores, specialty stores, and dealers. Search out objects that seem to have integrity: a sculpted bronze with fine features; a detailed wall hanging; a mirrorworked bedspread with astonishingly even stitches. Of course, you could not do better than to visit the bazaars of India itself, especially Chor Bazaar (thieves market) in Bombay and the state Emporia Complex in Delhi.

capturing the pageant

While writing this book I have never failed to be astonished and delighted by the innovation and skill of designers, craftspeople, and homemakers in my country, which are evident not only in the decoration of the wealthy homes of the cities, but also in the proud interiors of rural dwellings. Their styles emulate the many strong traditions that rely on a passion for beauty and harmony. To be inspired by the images of *India Style* is to understand and appreciate the rich pageantry of India, which will never cease to amaze.

Index

picture acknowledgments

All pictures by Bharath Ramamrutham except those on pages: 8, 9, Guy Dimond; 148, Julie Dixon; 4, 80, 144, Mark Luscombe Whyte; 35, 72, Mark Luscombe Whyte (Elizabeth Whiting Associates); 8, 10, 11, 14, 109, 114, 123, Porpoise, Bombay; 83, Fritz von Schulenberg (The Interior Archive); 12, 64, 79, 101, 137, Henry Wilson (The Interior Archive); 11, Harriet Podger; 11, Janie Airey (images of India); 157, Andreas von Einsiedel (Elizabeth Whiting Associates); 154, 155, Ray Main.

author's acknowledgments

·A big thank-you to Mr. Amberkar at the Rachna Sansad (School of Interior Design and Architecture) Bombay for opening their vast library to me, to my mother, Vimla Patil, for easing out the bottlenecks when I encountered them, to my colleague Bharath Ramamrutham for all those animated discussions revolving around a common love of India, and to Nitish and Arrush for being patient and understanding while I was writing this book. A very special thank-you to my daughter Saayli, who was born during the months when this book was taking shape and has had to share me with *India Style* ever since.

I also owe gratitude to Kyle Cathie, who comes up with questions that lead to exciting and unexplored avenues, to my editor Kate Oldfield, for her observations, notes, and queries about India and for her relentless attention to detail, and to my agent Teresa Chris, for always encouraging me to go for it!

publishers' acknowledgments

The publishers would like to acknowledge the extreme kindness that everyone who became involved with this book showed to the author and the photographer. They would especially like to thank everyone who opened up their homes in India for the camera- to Jamini Ahluwalia, Hari and Claudia Ajwani, Ratan Batliboi and the Hooseinallys, Anuradha Parekh Benegal, Romi Chopra, Dean D'Cruz, Rosa Costa Dias, Remo and Michelle Fernandes, Geeta P. Khandelwal, Jay Khanna, Rohini Khosla, Jean François Lesage and Patrick Savouret, Kamal Malik, R. Mohan, Ritu Nanda and Arjun Mangaldas, Aman Nath, Deepti Naval, Mita Parekh, Priti and Priya Paul, Gita Ram, Saroja Ramamrutham, Visalakshmi Ramaswamy, Wendell Rodricks and Jerome Marrel, Martand Singh, Sandy Starkman, Deborah Thiagarajan and the staff at Dakshinchitra, Venkat, Francis Wacziarg and the staff at Neemrana Fort Palace.

Nilaya Hermitage is a small designer hotel in Goa: tel +91 832 276793/4 and fax +91 832 276972

Thanks also to the following people for their invaluable advice and support: Kalpana Brijnath, Manika Chopra, Ashley Hicks, India Hicks, the Kaker family, Anuradha Mahindra, Neeru Nanda, Louise Nicholson, Penny Oliver, Vimla Patil, Saroja Ramamrutham, Vivek Sahni, Sheela Shahani and the staff of Inside Outside magazine, "Tiger" Singh, and Henry Wilson.

And thank you to Gerald, who was good-humored and helpful throughout, however many camera bags he had to carry.

bibliography

Dhamijia, Jasleen and Jain, Jyotindra (eds), *Handwoven Fabrics of India*

Dhamijlia, Jasleen, *Handwoven and Handworked Textiles of India*

Dongerkery, Kamala S., *Interior Decoration in India, Past and Present* (1973)

Fisher, Nora (ed), *Mud, Mirror and Thread—Folk Traditions of Rural India*

Kelkar, D.G., *Lamps of India*

Sharma, Jagdish, *Bhartiya Vastagyan* (1996)

Grewal, Royina, *In Rajasthan* (1997)